PEARSON LON

CORNERSTONE

3

PEARSON English Learning System

Anna Uhl Chamot

Jim Cummins

Sharroky Hollie

PEARSON

Upper Saddle River, New Jersey • Boston, Massachusetts • Chandler, Arizona • Glenview, Illinois

Published by
Pearson Education South Asia Pte Ltd
9 North Buona Vista Drive, #13-05/06, The Metropolis, Tower One
Singapore 138588

Pearson Education offices in Asia: Bangkok, Beijing, Ho Chi Minh City, Hong Kong, Jakarta, Kuala Lumpur, Manila, Seoul, Singapore, Taipei, Tokyo

Original edition, PEARSON LONGMAN CORNERSTONE 3, 9781428434745 by ANNA UHL CHAMOT, JIM CUMMINS AND SHARROKY HOLLIE published by Pearson Education, Inc., Copyright © 2013 Pearson Education, Inc.

Printed in Malaysia (CTP-VVP)

4   3   2   1
21 20 19 18

This impression 2018

ISBN: 978-981-3134-04-1

About the Authors

Anna Uhl Chamot is a professor of secondary education and a faculty advisor for ESL in George Washington University's Department of Teacher Preparation. She has been a researcher and teacher trainer in content-based, second-language learning, and language-learning strategies. She co-designed and has written extensively about the Cognitive Academic Language Learning Approach (CALLA) and spent seven years implementing the CALLA model in the Arlington Public Schools in Virginia.

Jim Cummins is the Canada Research Chair in the Department of Curriculum, Teaching, and Learning of the Ontario Institute for Studies in Education at the University of Toronto. His research focuses on literacy development in multilingual school contexts, as well as on the potential roles of technology in promoting language and literacy development. His recent publications include: *The International Handbook of English Language Teaching* (co-edited with Chris Davison) and *Literacy, Technology, and Diversity: Teaching for Success in Changing Times* (with Kristin Brown and Dennis Sayers).

Sharroky Hollie is an assistant professor in teacher education at California State University, Dominguez Hills. His expertise is in the field of professional development, African-American education, and second-language methodology. He is an urban literacy visiting professor at Webster University, St. Louis. Sharroky is the Executive Director of the Center for Culturally Responsive Teaching and Learning (CCRTL) and the co-founding director of the nationally-acclaimed Culture and Language Academy of Success (CLAS).

Consultants and Reviewers

Rebecca Anselmo
Sunrise Acres Elementary School
Las Vegas, NV

Ana Applegate
Redlands School District
Redlands, CA

Terri Armstrong
Houston ISD
Houston, TX

Jacqueline Avritt
Riverside County Office of Ed.
Hemet, CA

Mitchell Bobrick
Palm Beach County School
West Palm Beach, FL

Victoria Brioso-Saldala
Broward County Schools
Fort Lauderdale, FL

Brenda Cabarga Schubert
Creekside Elementary School
Salinas, CA

Joshua Ezekiel
Bardin Elementary School
Salinas, CA

Veneshia Gonzalez
Seminole Elementary School
Okeechobee, FL

Carolyn Grigsby
San Francisco Unified School District
San Francisco, CA

Julie Grubbe
Plainfield Consolidated Schools
Chicago, IL

Yasmin Hernandez-Manno
Newark Public Schools
Newark, NJ

Janina Kusielewicz
Clifton Public Schools/Bilingual Ed.
& Basic Skills Instruction Dept.
Clifton, NJ

Mary Helen Lechuga
El Paso ISD
El Paso, TX

Gayle P. Malloy
Randolph School District
Randolph, MA

Randy Payne
Patterson/Taft Elementaries
Mesa, AZ

Marcie L. Schnegelberger
Alisal Union SD
Salinas, CA

Lorraine Smith
Collier County Schools
Naples, FL

Shawna Stoltenborg
Glendale Elementary School
Glen Burnie, MD

Denise Tiffany
West High School
Iowa City, IO

Dear Student,

Welcome to Longman Cornerstone!

We wrote *Longman Cornerstone* to help you succeed in all your school studies. This program will help you learn the English language you need to study language arts, social studies, math, and science. You will learn how to speak to family members, classmates, and teachers in English.

Cornerstone includes a mix of many subjects. Each unit has four different readings that include some fiction (made-up) and nonfiction (true) articles, stories, songs, and poems. The readings will give you some of the tools you need to do well in all your subjects in school.

As you use this program, you will build on what you already know and learn new words, new information and facts, and take part in creative activities. The activities will help you improve your English skills.

Learning a language takes time, but just like learning to skateboard or learning to swim, it is fun!

We hope you enjoy *Longman Cornerstone* as much as we enjoyed writing it for you!

Good luck!

Anna Uhl Chamot
Jim Cummins
Sharroky Hollie

Contents

Communities

Reading 3: Literature/Personal Narrative

Meeting Challenges

Reading 3: Informational Text/Social Studies

Put It All Together

Animals at Home

Reading 3: Informational Text/Science

Great Ideas

Reading 3: Informational Text/Photo Essay

Neighbors in Space

Reading 1: Informational Text/Science

Reading 2: Literature/Myths

Reading 3: Informational Text/Biography

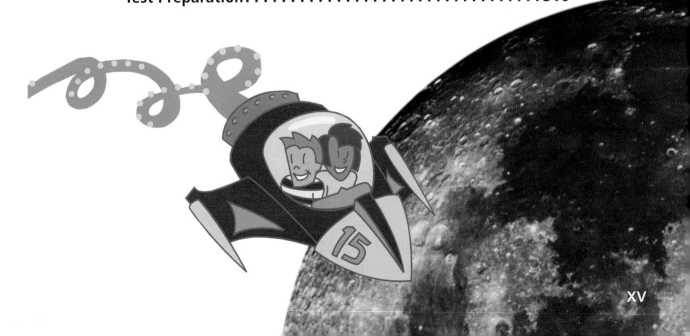

Arts Festivals

Reading 3: Informational Text/Newspaper Article

THE BIG QUESTION

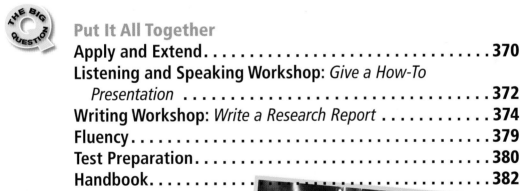

Communities

Your community is where you live with your family. It is where you play with your friends and go to school.

Reading

1 | Poem

Cool Hector

2 | Short Story

Making Friends

3 | Narrative

My Family

THE BIG Q QUESTION

What are some ways that communities are alike and different?

Listening and Speaking

You will talk about what children do in different communities. In the Listening and Speaking Workshop, you will play a descriptive guessing game.

Writing

You will practice descriptive writing. In the Writing Workshop, you will write a description of an event.

Quick Write

Think of another community you have visited. Write three sentences comparing that community to your community.

 DVD **VIEW AND RESPOND**
Talk about the poster for this unit. Then watch and listen to the video and answer the questions at LongmanCornerstone.com.

What do you know about communities?

Words to Know

Listen and repeat. Use these words to talk about people who work in your community.

| bus driver | police officer | mail carrier | teacher |

Work with a partner. Look up these words in a dictionary. Then ask and answer questions.

teaches us	protects us	brings us mail	drives a bus

Example: A: What does a <u>police officer</u> do?

            B: A <u>police officer protects us</u>.

Read the question. Write your response in your notebook.

What do you want to be when you grow up?

Make Connections

Copy the sentences into your notebook and complete them.

bus stop

police station

school

post office

1. Some police officers work at the _____ , and others work outside.

2. We go to _____ every day, and so do our teachers, the principal, and the rest of the staff.

3. We can give our mail to a mail carrier, or we can take it to the _____ .

4. You can catch a bus at a bus station or at a _____ .

What about you?

Talk with a partner. Talk about other jobs in your community. Where do the people who do those jobs work? What do they do?

Kids' Stories from around the World Audio

Illinois, U.S.A.

Chile

Chris

My family and I live in a suburb. The suburb is near a big city in Illinois. A suburb has many houses. My friends and I take the yellow bus to go to school. In the afternoon, we do our homework. Then all the children play outside.

Lucia

My family and I live in a small town in the Andes. The Andes are mountains in Chile. There is no school in my town. I go to a school in another town. It is thirty miles away! The ride to school is long, but I love living in the mountains.

Gen

I live in a big city called Shanghai. Shanghai is in China. My family lives in a tall apartment building. My sister and I take the bus to go to school. The city is busy in the morning.

China

South Africa

Mandisa

I am from South Africa. I live on my family's farm. We grow strawberries. There are other farms near us. All the children get together in the morning to go to school. We help around the farm, too.

What about you?

1. What kind of community do you live in?

2. How do you get to school? Share your story.

What You Will Learn

Reading

- Vocabulary building: *Context, phonics*

- Reading strategy: *Understand character*

- Text type: *Literature (poem)*

Grammar

Simple present: *be* verbs

Writing

Describe a person

These words will help you understand the reading.

Key Words

neat

street

luck

flower

mail

Key Words

Cool Hector is a poem about a boy going around his neighborhood.

Words in Context Audio

1 This bike is so neat!

2 There are a lot of people on the street.

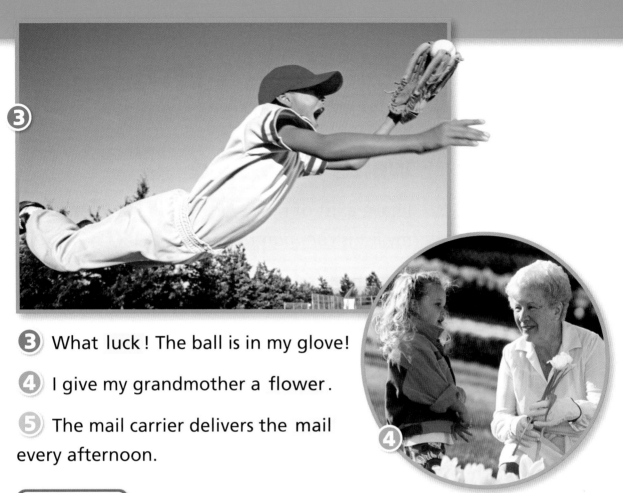

③ What luck ! The ball is in my glove!

④ I give my grandmother a flower.

⑤ The mail carrier delivers the mail every afternoon.

Practice

Create a vocabulary notebook.

- Divide your page into three columns: the new words, their definitions, and drawings of the words when possible.
- Test yourself by covering one of the columns.

Make Connections

Hector likes to talk to people in his community. What do you like to do in your community? Why? Discuss. Use some of the key words as you speak.

3

These words will help you talk about the reading.

Academic Words

item
single piece or thing

purchase
buy

Academic Words

Words in Context

I have a list of new words. The first **item** on my list is *communities.*

You can **purchase** a book at a bookstore.

[Practice]

Write the sentences in your notebook. Choose an academic word to complete each sentence.

1. We go to the post office to ____ stamps for our mail.

2. I have a list of things to do today. The first ____ on my list is to walk my dog.

[Apply]

Write the answers in your notebook. Use the academic words. Then ask and answer with a partner.

1. What is one **item** your family usually buys at the store?

2. Do you usually get books from the library, or do you **purchase** them?

Phonics

Short Vowels

The **vowels** are *a, e, i, o,* and *u.* The other letters are called **consonants**. The words in the chart have short vowels. Listen. Then read each word aloud.

| can | bed | sit | top | bus |

Rule

A word may have a short vowel when:
- the word has just one vowel.
- the word has a consonant before and after the vowel.

c a t   p u p
C V C   C V C

Practice

Work with a partner. Take turns.

- Read the sentences.
- Find the words with the CVC pattern.

   1. Gus drives the bus.

   2. The cat is big.

   3. The girls sit on the bed.

   4. Do not pick up the pup.

5

LITERATURE

Poem

More About

Why is each person an important part of the community?

 Listen to the Audio.
Listen for the general meaning. Use the pictures to help you understand the selection.

Reading Strategy

Understand Character

As you read, think about the main character, Hector:

- What does he do?
- What kind of person is he? Find clues.

Listen as your teacher models the reading strategy.

Cool Hector

by Vivian Binnamin
illustrated by Ellen Joy Sasaki

Hector skips along the street.
He thinks, "This city is SO neat!"
To lots of people on his way,
he says, "¡Hola! How's your day?"

Reading Skill

The words *street* and *neat* are key words for this reading.

When Hector walks right by the park,
a big, black dog begins to bark.
Hector sees a disk fly by.
He catches it on his first try.

Hector goes into the store,
picks out an orange and then one more.
He sees a pretty flower to buy.
Hector's really quite a **guy**!

Reading Skill

To understand the word *guy*, read the definition below.

———————————

guy   boy or man

Before You Go On   How does Hector feel about the city? How do you know?

Hector sees the mail truck.

"Oh!" he says aloud. "What luck!"

Ms. Rodriguez drops some mail.

Hector's there. He does not fail.

Hector likes to ride the bus,

so he hops the Number Ten with Gus.

Gus lets Hector close the door.

(Hector did it once before.)

Hector buys something to eat,
choosing something cool and sweet.
Then he gives his mom the **ice**.
Hector's really very nice.

---

ice   frozen food made from fruit

W B
6–8

Reading Strategy

Understand Character

Looking for clues can help you learn about a character.

- What clues help you learn what Hector is like?

- How did looking for clues help you learn about Hector?

Think It Over

1. **Recall**   What **items** does Hector **purchase**?

2. **Comprehend**   How does Hector help people in his community?

3. **Analyze**   How do you think people feel about Hector?

Learning Strategies

Understand Character

A **character** is a person in a story or poem. You can learn about characters by what they say or do.

Practice

Read each sentence. Then choose the word that tells what Hector is like.

a. helpful	**b.** busy
c. nice	**d.** friendly

1. ___ Hector says "¡Hola!" to people.

2. ___ Hector walks by a park, goes to a store, and rides the bus.

3. ___ Hector picks up the mail.

4. ___ Hector gives his mom the ice.

16   UNIT 1

Use a Character Web

You can use a Character Web to tell
what a person is like.

Copy this Character Web. Tell what Hector does.
Tell what Hector is like. The first one is done for you.

Hector says
"¡Hola!" to people
he meets. Hector
is friendly.

Hector_____.

Hector is_____.

Hector

Hector_____.

Hector is_____.

Hector_____.

Hector is_____.

1. Which actions tell you that Hector is helpful?

2. How do you know that Hector likes to be busy?

3. How do you know that Hector is happy?

9

Retell the poem to a partner.
You can refer to the pictures as
you speak.

Extension

Utilize   What do you like to
do in your community? Create
a picture that shows what you
like to do. Share your drawing.

Grammar

Simple Present: *be* Verbs

The *be* **verb** tells what something is or is like.

> He **is** Hector.

> We **are** at school.

This chart shows the different forms of *be*. On the right are contractions, or short forms, of the subject and *be*.

Subject	*be*	
I	am	
You	are	nice.
He / She / It	is	
We / They	are	

Contractions
I'm
You're
He's / She's / It's
We're / They're

To make **negative sentences**, add *not* after *be*.

Affirmative	Negative
Hector **is** there. ⟶	Hector **is not** there.

is not = **isn't**
are not = **aren't**

To make **Yes-No** and **Wh-questions**, put the *be* verb before the subject.

> **Is** Hector there?
> Yes, he **is**.

> **Where is** Hector?
> He **is** at the park.

Practice

Add the correct form of *be*.
Write the sentences.

Example: The flower <u>is</u> pretty.

1. You ____ quite a guy.

2. The dogs ____ neat.

3. We ____ in the park.

4. Where ____ the mail?

5. ____ your mom and dad nice?

Apply

Work with a partner. Ask and answer the questions.
Use *be* verbs in your answers.

Example: A: How old are you?

            B: I'm eight years old.

- How old are you?
- What is your name?
- When is your birthday?
- Where are your pencils?

- Is your notebook new?
- Are you from Mexico?
- Who is our teacher?
- What are the other students' names?

10

Grammar Check ✓

Name some *be* verbs.

Writing

Ongoing Writing Skills Practice

Describe a Person

When you describe a person, you can say what the person looks like, or you can focus on the person's actions.

Writing Prompt

Write a paragraph describing a person. Tell about the person's actions. Say what these actions show about the person. Be sure to use *be* verbs correctly.

❶ Prewrite

G.O. 149

Choose a person to write about. Think about this person's actions. What do the person's actions tell you about him or her? List your ideas in a T-chart.

A student named Maria listed her ideas like this:

MY MOTHER	
HER ACTIONS	WHAT HER ACTIONS SHOW
smiles a lot	friendly
visits our neighbor	kind
spends time with me	patient and loving

❷ Draft

Use your T-chart to help you write a first draft.

- Keep in mind your purpose—to describe a person.
- Tell what the person's actions show about him or her.

❸ Revise

Reread your draft. Look for places where it needs improvement. Use the Writing Checklist to help you find problems. Then revise your draft.

❹ Edit

Check your work for errors. Use the Peer Review Checklist on page 402.

❺ Publish

Make a clean copy of your final draft. Share it with the class. Save your work. You will need it for the Writing Workshop.

Here is Maria's description:

Writing Checklist

Ideas

✓ I told what Mom's actions show about her.

✓ I expressed my ideas clearly.

Conventions

✓ I used the verb *be* correctly.

✓ Pronouns and verbs agree.

Maria Gonzalez

My mother is friendly. She says hi to people and smiles at them. Our neighbor, Mrs. King, lives alone. My mother visits her every afternoon. Mrs. King says my mother is the kindest woman she knows. My mother spends a lot of time with me. She and I talk a lot. She is very patient and loving. She's a great mom!

11–12

Prepare to Read

What You Will Learn

Reading

■ Vocabulary building: *Context, phonics*

■ Reading strategy: *Preview*

■ Text type: *Literature (short story)*

Grammar
Simple present

Writing

Describe a typical summer day

These words will help you understand the reading.

Key Words

dessert

friend

fold

mix

Key Words

Making Friends is a story about two new children in a school.

Words in Context

1 Which dessert would you like to eat?

2 Meg likes to run with her friend, Tom. What do you like to do with a friend?

2

3 Yuki likes to fold paper.
She makes paper birds.

4 Juan can mix things.
He helps his grandfather cook.

Practice

Make flashcards to help you memorize the words.

- Write a key word on the front.
- On the back, write the meaning.

Make Connections

Families may visit a new place. Do you remember a time when you were in a new place? Describe how you felt. Use some of the key words as you speak.

Speaking Skills

If you don't know how to say something, ask your teacher for help.

13

These words will help you talk about the reading.

Academic Words

create
make something

task
job that must be done

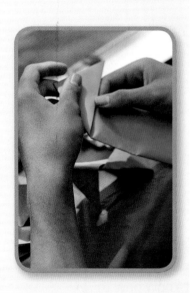

Academic Words

Words in Context

Our art teacher shows us how to **create** fun things.

When it is time to clean up, our teacher gives everyone a **task**. I have to put away the books.

Practice

Write the sentences in your notebook. Choose an academic word to complete each sentence.

1. My mother can _____ beautiful pictures on the computer.

2. Tomorrow we are going to do a group project. My _____ is to bring a newspaper to school.

Apply

Write the answers in your notebook. Use the academic words. Then ask and answer with a partner.

1. Where do you **create** art? At home? At school? At other places?

2. What **tasks** do you enjoy? What **tasks** do you not enjoy?

14

Phonics

Long Vowels with Silent *e*

Each vowel can stand for more than one sound.
Listen. Then read each word aloud.

a		i		o		u	
hat	hate	hid	hide	hop	hope	hug	huge
can	cane	lick	like	not	note	cub	cube

- The words in the gray boxes have short vowels.
- The words in the white boxes have long vowels.
- Listen again. Which vowels say their own names?

Rule

The vowel is long when it is followed by a consonant
and the letter *e*. The letter *e* is silent.

Short Vowel	Long Vowel
m a d	m a d e
C V C	C V C e

Practice

Work with a partner. Take turns.

- Write two new CVCe words for each vowel: *a*, *i*, *o*, and *u*.
- Read the words to a partner.

15

LITERATURE

Short Story

More About

How is it helpful to have different people in your community?

 Listen to the Audio.
Listen for the general meaning. Use the pictures to help you understand the selection.

Reading Strategy

Preview

To preview means to look at the pages before you read.

- Read the title.
- Look at the illustrations.
- Try to predict what the text is about.

Listen as your teacher models the reading strategy.

Making Friends

by Dan Ahearn
illustrated by Laurie Keller

The girls and boys in Miss Jones's class are from many **different** countries. But every family does fun things. Girls and boys can teach these fun things to friends.

Kate teaches a song to Juan. Juan tells a story to Kate. Maria shows Ben how to play a game. Most of the girls and boys are smiling. They are having fun.

But Hana and Carlos are sad.

—————————————————————————————

different   not like something or someone else

Before You Go On   What fun things do the girls and boys teach each other?

Hana just came to this school. She is from **Japan**. Hana does not have a friend yet.

Carlos just came here. He is from Mexico. Carlos does not have a friend yet.

Miss Jones tells Carlos to sit by Hana. She asks Hana to teach a fun thing to Carlos. Hana says she can make paper animals. Her mother showed her how. Carlos thinks that is a fun thing to do.

Japan   country in Asia

Hana takes out some paper. She makes a paper crane. A crane is a bird. Carlos asks Hana to show him how to make a paper crane. Hana shows him how to fold the paper. Carlos makes a paper crane, too.

Now what can Carlos do? Carlos can make a dessert. But he needs his mother to help. He will teach Hana how to make a dessert.

Before You Go On

What special item does Hana **create**?

Hana goes to Carlos's house. His mother gives Carlos the things he needs. He mixes them. Carlos shows Hana how to make the dessert. Hana mixes the things, too.

His mother cooks the dessert. Carlos and Hana watch. It is fun making dessert! Soon, the dessert is ready. Hana tastes the dessert. It is so good!

At school, they will show other girls and boys what they learned.

Hana shows the dessert they made. Carlos showed her how to make the dessert.

Carlos shows a paper crane he made. Hana showed him how to make the paper crane.

The other girls and boys taste the dessert. They make paper cranes. Carlos and Hana show them how.

Hana and Carlos can do new things. All of the girls and boys can do new things, too. Hana and Carlos now have many friends.

16–18

Reading Strategy

Preview

- Did previewing help you predict what the story would be about?
- How else did previewing help you understand the story?

Think It Over

1. **Recall**   What **task** does the teacher give Hana?

2. **Comprehend**   What do Hana and Carlos have in common?

3. **Analyze**   Why are Hana and Carlos happy at the end of the story?

Learning Strategies

Sequence of Events

Events are things that happen in a story. Events happen in a certain order. This order is called the **sequence**.

Read these events from *Making Friends*. Write the events in the order that they happen in the story.

- Carlos and Hana are sad.
- Carlos shows Hana how to make a dessert.
- Carlos and Hana share what they learned with the other girls and boys.
- Carlos and Hana watch Carlos's mother cook the dessert.
- Hana shows Carlos how to make a paper bird.
- Hana goes to Carlos's house.

Use a Sequence Chart

A Sequence Chart can help you think about
events in the order that they happen.

Copy the chart. Answer the questions.

1.		2.		3.		4.
Hana and Carlos don't have friends.	▶	Hana shows Carlos how to make a paper bird.	▶		▶	Hana and Carlos share what they learned with the other girls and boys.

1. Which event should be in box 3?

  a. Hana and Carlos are sad.

  b. Hana shows Carlos how to make a dessert.

  c. Hana and Carlos have fun with their new friends.

  d. Carlos shows Hana how to make a dessert.

2. Add a new box at the end. Choose an event to add.

  a. Hana and Carlos are sad.

  b. Hana and Carlos become friends with the
  other girls and boys.

  c. Carlos's mother cooks the dessert.

  d. Carlos needs his mother's help.

**Retell the story to a partner. Use some
of the key words as you speak.**

19

Extension

Utilize Think of something
you know how to make. Teach
a partner how to make it. Then
switch roles and follow your
partner's directions.

Grammar

Simple Present

Verbs in the simple present tell what usually happens. They change form to agree with the subject of the sentence.

> **Hana goes** to school.

> **I go** to school.

This chart shows the two forms of present verbs.
If the subject is *he*, *she*, or *it*, add *-s* or *-es* to the verb.

Subject	Verb	Verb
I / You / We / They	fold	mix
He / She / It	folds	mixes

To make **negative sentences**, add *do not* or *does not* before the plain form of the verb.

> Affirmative   Negative
> She smiles. ⟶ She **does not smile.**

> do not = **don't**
> does not = **doesn't**

To make **questions**, use *do* or *does* before the subject.

> **Does** Carlos **help** his mother?
> Yes, he **does**.

> **Do** you **help** your mother?
> Yes, I **do**.

Practice

Circle the correct form of the verb.
Write the sentences.

Example: Carlos (mix, (mixes)) things.

1. The teacher (ask, asks) questions.

2. I (fold, folds) the paper in half.

3. Hana (create, creates) a new tradition.

4. Her friend does not (smile, smiles).

5. Do your friends (like, likes) dessert?

Apply

Work with a partner. Ask and answer the questions.
Use the simple present in your answers.

Example: A: Do you walk to school?
B: Yes, I walk to school.

- Do you walk to school?
- Do your friends live near you?
- Does your father fix things?
- Do you like cold weather?
- Does your mother watch television?
- Do you help at home?
- Does your teacher smile a lot?
- Do you like dessert?

20

Grammar Check ✓

Make a sentence using the **simple present.**

Writing

Ongoing Writing Skills Practice

Describe a Summer Day

When you describe an event, you tell who is there and what they do.

Writing Prompt

Write a paragraph describing a typical summer day. Tell about who you are with and what you do. Be sure to use the simple present correctly.

❶ Prewrite G.O. 144

Choose a typical summer day to write about. Who are you with? What things do you do? List your ideas in a graphic organizer.

A student named Margarita listed her ideas like this:

My Summer Days

Abuela, Liliana, and I go to the park.

Liliana and I play. Abuela sits and watches us.

The ice cream truck comes. We buy ice cream.

❷ Draft

Use your graphic organizer to help you write a first draft.

- Keep in mind your purpose—to describe.
- Include details about people and actions.

❸ Revise

Reread your draft. Look for places where it needs improvement. Use the Writing Checklist to help you find problems. Then revise your draft.

❹ Edit

Check your work for errors. Use the Peer Review Checklist on page 402.

❺ Publish

Make a clean copy of your final draft. Share it with the class. Save your work. You will need it for the Writing Workshop.

Here is Margarita's description:

> Margarita Hernandez
>
> In the summer I go to the park near my apartment. My sister, Liliana, and I play. Our grandmother, Abuela, sits on a bench and watches us. Later, the ice cream truck arrives. Liliana and I race to be first. I ask for chocolate. Liliana's favorite is strawberry. As we walk home, I smell flowers and grass. I love these summer days.

Writing Checklist

Ideas

✓ I included interesting details.

✓ I expressed my ideas clearly.

Conventions

✓ I used verbs in the simple present correctly.

✓ Subjects and verbs agree.

WB
21–22

Key Words

What You Will Learn

Reading

- Vocabulary building: *Context, word study*

- Reading strategy: *Make connections*

- Text type: *Literature (personal narrative)*

Grammar

Nouns: singular and plural

Writing

Describe a family celebration

These words will help you understand the reading.

Key Words

celebrate

crowd

company

weekend

gathers

In *My Family,* a girl describes her family. She tells what her family does together.

Words in Context

Audio

1 I like to celebrate my birthday. It makes me feel special.

2 Many children are in one place. These children make a crowd.

3 We like to have company for dinner.

4 The weekend is Saturday and Sunday. We do not have school. We work in the community garden.

5 All the family gathers around to hear Grandmother sing.

Practice

Make flash cards to help you memorize the words.
- Write a word on the front.
- On the back, write a sentence, but leave a blank where the key word should be.

Make Connections

In the story *My Family*, a girl tells what she likes to do with her family. Describe what you like to do with your family. Use some of the key words as you speak.

23

These words will help you talk about the reading.

Academic Words

contribute
give something

similar
almost the same, but not quite

Academic Words

Words in Context

My family likes to **contribute** old books to the town library.
Every month, the lunch menu at our school is **similar** to the month before.

Practice

Write the sentences in your notebook. Choose an academic word to complete each sentence.

1. Everyone in the class has to _____ something to the party. I'm going to bring juice.

2. Pink is _____ to the color red, but pink is lighter.

Apply

Write the answers in your notebook. Use the academic words. Then ask and answer with a partner.

1. When it is time to clean up the classroom, how do you **contribute**?

2. How are you **similar** to a family member or another important person in your life?

Word Study

Use a Dictionary

Read this dictionary entry.

> **gath • er** (gathər) verb **1** to bring or come together <gather your things>. **2** to gain little by little <gather speed>. **3** to come to a conclusion <gather that you are going>.
> **gathered, gathering.**

Practice

Work with a partner.

- The entry for **gather** has more than one meaning.
- Find the meaning that makes sense in each sentence.

1. Anna started to **gather** speed on her bike.

2. **Gather** your books together.

3. I **gather** that this reading is about a family.

W B
25

More About

THE BIG QUESTION

How is your family a community?

 Listen to the Audio.

Listen for the general meaning. Use the pictures to help you understand the selection.

Reading Strategy

Make Connections

As you read, think about your family.

- What does your family celebrate?
- Who comes when you celebrate?
- What special things do you do?

Listen as your teacher models the reading strategy.

My Family

by Hanna Jamal
illustrated by Kathryn Mitter

My family likes to celebrate. We like to be together.

Monday through Friday, everyone is busy. We go to school. We go to work. We do homework. We do **chores**.

But on the weekend, we get together. And whenever my family gets together, we always have a good time.

---

chores   jobs that you have to do often

I live in Madison, Wisconsin, with my parents and my brother. My grandparents live in Madison, too. My aunts and uncles live in Milwaukee, Wisconsin. On some weekends, we drive to Milwaukee to visit them. On other weekends, they drive to Madison to visit us.

I like it when we get together. We talk, laugh, and play games. There is **plenty** of food to eat. There is plenty of noise! You can tell that everyone is happy to be together.

---

plenty   a lot

Before You Go On   When does the family get together?

Sometimes, we celebrate a special day. Today we celebrate my grandmother's birthday. We all work together to plan her party.

My mother bakes a cake, and my cousins and I put up **streamers**. We each have a gift to give to my grandmother.

We sing the birthday song. My grandfather smiles. He sings, too.

---

streamers   long, thin colored paper

There are a lot of **candles** on my grandmother's cake! We watch her blow out the candles. We ask her what she wished for, but she will not say.

My grandmother has fun at her birthday party. She is happy to have the family together.

I think I know what she wished for. Her wish is to have many more family celebrations.

---

candles   sticks of wax that burn and give light

Before You Go On   How does the family show their love for the grandmother?

When the weather is warm, friends join our family celebrations. Company gathers in our yard. Neighbors, friends, and family come over. There is a big crowd.

Everyone brings something to the party. There is plenty of food. Dad cooks. Mom makes **salad**. We drink **lemonade**. We eat dessert.

We laugh and talk. We play games and have fun. You can tell that we are having a good time. I like to see everyone together.

---

salad   a dish of raw leafy vegetables

lemonade   a sweet drink made from lemon juice

At last, the party is over. The neighbors go home. Our friends go home, too. The aunts, uncles, and cousins say goodbye. My grandmother and grandfather say good night.

Now it is quiet. But next weekend, we will have another celebration. We will see the whole family together again.

WB
26–28

Reading Strategy

Make Connections

- How is your family **similar** to the one in the story?

- How is your family different from the one in the story?

- How did making connections help you understand the story?

Think It Over

1. **Recall**   Where does the family have celebrations?

2. **Comprehend**   How do friends and family members **contribute** to the parties?

3. **Analyze**   How do friends and family members feel about each other? Give examples.

A Family Tree

Grandmother ▶
She is my
mother's mother.

◀ **Grandfather**
He is my
mother's father.

▲ **Aunt**
She is my uncle's wife.

▲ **Uncle**
He is my mother's brother.

▲ **Mother**
This is my mother.

Amelia ▶
Hi! I'm Amelia.
This is my
family tree.

▲ **Cousin**
He is my aunt and uncle's son.

Grandmother ▶
She is my
father's mother.

◀ **Grandfather**
He is my
father's father.

◀ **Father**
This is my father.

Activity to Do

These two pages use words
and pictures to tell you about
family trees.

- Think about your family.
- Make a family tree using
  pictures and words.
- Post your family tree in
  your classroom.

▲ **Brother**
This is my brother.

▲ **Sister**
This is my sister.

Learning Strategies

Make Connections

Your family may be like another family. It may be different. You can ask yourself questions to learn about families.

- How are my family celebrations **similar** to the celebrations in the story?
- How are my family celebrations different from the celebrations in the story?

Practice

Look back at the story. Answer the questions.

1. What do the aunts and uncles do at family celebrations?
2. How does the family **celebrate** the grandmother's birthday?
3. What does the family do when **company** comes over?

Use a T-Chart

You can use a T-chart to show how things are alike and different.

 G.O. 149

Copy this chart. Answer the questions below. Tell about the family in the story. Tell about your own family.

Story Family	Your Family
1. They get together on the weekend.	1.
2. Her aunts, uncles, cousins. . .	2.
3.	3.
4.	4.

1. When do you get together?

2. Who comes to the celebrations?

3. What do different family members do?

4. What do you do with family and friends?

Summarize the story for a partner.

W B

29

Extension

Utilize   Think of a special thing you do with your family. Describe this to a partner. Tell who is there. Tell what you do.

Grammar

Nouns: Singular and Plural

A **singular noun** names one person, place, or thing.

A **plural noun** names two or more people, places, or things.

most nouns, add **-s**	crowd ⟶ crowd**s**
nouns ending in *-s, -ch, -sh,* or *-x,* add **-es**	dress ⟶ dress**es** wish ⟶ wish**es**
nouns ending in vowel + consonant + *-y,* change **-y** to **-i** and add **-es**	family ⟶ famil**ies** baby ⟶ bab**ies**
irregular nouns, **look them up in the dictionary**	child ⟶ **children** person ⟶ **people**

Before nouns for specific people, places, or things, use **the**.

> Let's sing **the** birthday song.

Before a nonspecific person, place, or thing, use *a* or *an*.
Use *an* before words that begin with a **vowel** or a **vowel sound**.

> I have **a banana**. My sister has **an orange**.

Use **this** or **that** with singular verbs. Use **these** or **those**
with plural verbs.

> **This cake** is delicious. **That cake** is old.
> **These cakes** are delicious. **Those cakes** are old.

Practice

Choose the correct form of the noun.
Write the sentences.

Example: I see many (person, people)
in the park.

I see many people in the park.

1. Are they your (aunt, aunts)?

2. We have a (party, parties) today.

3. Look at all the (box, boxes)!

4. You have an (hour, hours) to play.

5. Grandfather has a (smile, smiles) on his face.

Apply

Work with a partner. Ask and answer the questions.
Use singular and plural nouns in your answers.

Example: A: How many pencils do you have?

B: I have two pencils.

- How many pencils do you have?
- What do you have in your backpack?
- How many people are in this room?
- What do you have in your room at home?
- How many children are there in your family?
- What do you have on your desk?

30

Grammar Check ✓

Name three *plural nouns* and three *singular nouns.*

Writing

Describe a Family Celebration

There are many ways to describe events. One way is to describe everything you remember about a special event.

Writing Prompt

Write a paragraph describing a family celebration. Tell about who is there and what everyone does. Be sure to use singular and plural nouns correctly.

❶ Prewrite

G.O.
153

Choose a family celebration to write about. Who is there? What does everyone do to prepare? List your ideas in a word web.

A student named Yuki listed his ideas like this:

❷ Draft

Use your word web to help you write a first draft.

• Keep in mind your purpose—to describe.

• Include details about the people and what they do.

❸ Revise

Reread your draft. Look for places where it needs improvement. Use the Writing Checklist to help you find problems. Then revise your draft.

❹ Edit

Check your work for errors. Use the Peer Review Checklist on page 402.

❺ Publish

Make a clean copy of your final draft. Share it with the class. Save your work. You will need it for the Writing Workshop.

Here is Hideo's description of a family celebration:

Hideo Furuya

Every year, we have a birthday party for my grandfather. The whole family works together. My cousins put flowers around the house. My aunts make a beautiful cake. My sisters put candles on the cake. My brothers put up balloons in the living room. Then we hide. We hear my grandfather's feet on the front porch. When he opens the door, we yell, "Surprise!"

WB
31–32

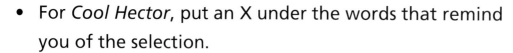

Apply and Extend

Link the Readings

Copy the chart into your notebook. Read the words in the top row.

- For *Cool Hector*, put an X under the words that remind you of the selection.

- Repeat the same activity for the other readings.

	Informational text	Literature	Being nice to neighbors	Planning a party
Cool Hector				
Making Friends				
My Family				

Discussion

1. How are Hector and Hana **similar**?

2. In the story *Making Friends,* how do Carlos and Hana get to know their classmates?

3. In the story *My Family*, how do the family members and friends **contribute** to the celebrations?

What are some ways that communities are alike and different?

Listening Skills

If someone is speaking too quickly, you can ask "Can you speak more slowly, please?"

Projects

Your teacher will help you choose one of these projects.

Written	Oral	Visual/Active
Lists	**Conversation**	**Postcards**
List three things you like about your community and three things that you wish you could change.	Talk with someone who moved from one community to another. How are the places alike and different?	Make a postcard that shows the community in *Cool Hector.* Make a postcard that shows your community.
Letters	**Town Song**	**Comic Strip**
Write letters between you and a character in one of the stories. Tell each other about your communities.	Write new words to *The Wheels on the Bus* to create the song *The People in Our Town.* Teach others to sing it.	Find out about a community in another country. Create a comic strip that shows what children do there.

Further Reading

For more projects visit
LongmanCornerstone.com

My Home, Margaret Lo
> This Penguin Young Reader® is a collection of stories, fun activities, and fascinating facts about different homes around the world.

Uptown, Bryan Collier
> A young person from Harlem takes readers on a tour of his neighborhood. He describes what life is like in his New York City community.

33–34

Play a Description Guessing Game

You are going to describe a place in the community. Then you will listen as your classmates talk about a place in the community.

❶ Prepare

A. Choose a place in your community. You will describe this place, but you won't name it. Your classmates will guess the place.

B. Close your eyes. Visualize the place you are going to describe. Write down some details.

> This place is in the city. There are many animals in this place. The animals are not pets like dogs or cats. I go to this place on the weekend with my family. I usually visit the area with the pandas. What is the name of this place?

❷ Practice

Practice your presentation five times or more. Practice in front of your family or friends. If possible, record your presentation. Then listen to yourself. How do you sound? Record yourself again and try to improve.

❸ Present

As you speak, do the following:

- Don't be nervous. Have fun.
- Describe a place in the community. Ask your classmates to guess what place you are describing.

As you listen, do the following:

- Listen quietly to your classmates. Don't call out any guesses. Wait until your classmates ask for them.
- If you don't understand something a speaker says, you can say, "Excuse me. Could you repeat that, please?"

❹ Evaluate

After you speak, answer these questions:
- ✓ Did you understand the game rules?
- ✓ Did you choose good description words?

After you listen, answer these questions:
- ✓ Did you understand the speaker?
- ✓ Did you guess the place?

Speaking Skills

Use informal language when playing a game. *Informal language* is the language you use when you speak with family, friends, and classmates.

Listening Skills

Take notes as you listen. Taking notes helps you to listen attentively.

Writing Workshop

Describe an Event

Writing Prompt

Write an essay describing an event. Describe what happened in the order that it happened. Include specific words and vivid details.

❶ Prewrite

Review the writing you have done for this unit. Now choose a topic. Think of an event that was interesting. List the details of the event in a graphic organizer.

A student named David listed his ideas like this:

G.O. 144

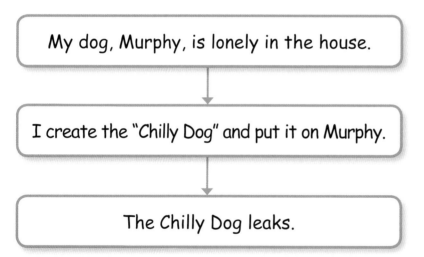

My dog, Murphy, is lonely in the house.

I create the "Chilly Dog" and put it on Murphy.

The Chilly Dog leaks.

Listening Skills

Writing an essay is a process. Listen carefully to your teacher's instructions and requests.

❷ Draft

Use your graphic organizer to write a first draft.

- Keep in mind your purpose—to describe an event.
- Include details that help the reader create a mental picture.

❸ Revise

Read your draft. Look for places where the writing needs improvement. Use the Writing Checklist to help you find problems. Then revise your draft.

Six Traits of Writing Checklist

✓ **Ideas**
Are all of my sentences related to the topic?

✓ **Organization**
Are my ideas in the right order?

✓ **Voice**
Is my writing lively?

✓ **Word Choice**
Do my words create pictures in the reader's mind?

✓ **Sentence Fluency**
Did I use different kinds of sentences?

✓ **Conventions**
Are my verbs in the correct tense?

Here is how David revised his essay:

David Mendez

The Chilly Dog

Every summer my dog , Murphy, stays inside because of the heat. He gets lonely, and I feel bad. But this year I can make the "Chilly Dog."

First, I cut holes in an old vest. Next, I put plastic bags full of ice into the holes. Then I put the vest on Murphy.

Revised to correct plural form.

Murphy is happy. But then the ice begins to melt. Water leaks out of the bags. My invention does not work so well after all. Murphy does not mind. He is a good dog.

Revised to correct verb agreement.

④ Edit

Check your work for errors. Trade papers with a partner. Use the Peer Review Checklist.

⑤ Publish

Make a clean copy of your final draft. Share it with the class.

35–36

Peer Review Checklist

✓ The details of the event are in order.

✓ The writing is interesting.

✓ Pronouns and verbs agree.

SPELLING TIP

Add -es to 3rd person singular verbs in the simple present if the verb ends in -s, -ch, -sh, or -x. If the verb ends in y, change y to i, then add -es.

Listen to the sentences. Pay attention to the groups of words. Read aloud.

1. Hector likes to visit many places in his community.
2. New friends can teach each other new things.
3. Many families like to celebrate special days together.

Work in pairs. Take turns reading the passage below aloud for one minute. Count the number of words you read.

Making Friends tells about a classroom of children from all	10
over the world. The teacher wants them to teach each other	21
something fun. Hana is from Japan and Carlos is from Mexico.	32
They are sad because they don't know anyone yet.	41
In class, Hana shows Carlos how to make a bird from paper.	53
Carlos folds paper and makes a crane. Carlos wants to show	64
Hana how to make a dessert at his house. Hana and Carlos make	77
a good dessert.	80

With your partner, find the words that slowed you down.

- Practice saying each word and then say the sentence each word is in.
- Then take turns reading the text again. Count the number of words you read.

WB

37

Test Preparation

Taking Tests

You will often take tests that help show what you know. Follow these tips to improve your test-taking skills.

Coaching Corner

Answering Test Questions

- Sometimes you will answer test questions that are based on reading selections. At other times, you will use a picture or a chart to help you answer a question.

- Before you answer a question based on a picture, read the question carefully. Be sure you understand what the question is asking. Study the picture closely before you choose an answer.

- When questions are based on a reading selection, first read the selection, then read the questions. After you choose an answer, review the reading passage again to make sure your answer is correct.

Read the following test sample. Study the tips in the box.

WB
39–40

Read and answer the question below.

1 This is a _____.

   A turtle
   B clock
   C flower
   D baseball

Tip

✓ Study the picture to find the answer.

Read the selection. Then answer the questions.

Station #39

Each year our class takes a field trip to visit the fire station. We all climb inside the fire truck and explore. Rick pretends to turn on the siren. Jesse tries on a firefighter's hat. Rosa plays with the fire station's dog. Chris slides down the fire pole. Then, the fire chief tells us about fire safety. We always enjoy our visit to the fire station!

2 Who is Jesse?

   A the fire chief
   B a dog
   C the author
   D a student in the class

Tips

✓ To answer Question 2, look for the people doing the action in most of the sentences.

✓ Think about the meaning of each of the answer choices. Which one makes sense?

3 In the first sentence, the word <u>takes</u> means —

   F goes on
   G plans
   H grabs
   J walks to

Meeting Challenges

Solving problems and trying new things can be a challenge. People work hard to meet challenges.

Reading

1 | Play

The Rabbit and the Lion

2 | Fable

The Contest

3 | Social Studies

Sharing a Garden

THE BIG QUESTION

All of us have challenges at times. How can people meet challenges?

Listening and Speaking

You will talk about any challenges you face and what you do to meet those challenges. In the Listening and Speaking Workshop, you will perform a skit.

Writing

You will practice narrative writing. In the Writing Workshop, you will write a story.

Quick Write

Make a list of three challenges students face at the beginning of each school year.

DVD **VIEW AND RESPOND**
Talk about the poster for this unit. Then watch and listen to the video and answer the questions at LongmanCornerstone.com.

What do you know about meeting challenges?

Words to Know

Listen and repeat. Use these words to talk about meeting challenges.

practice   study   rehearse   train

Practice

Work with a partner. Look up these words in a dictionary. Then ask and answer questions.

| the race | the test | the school play | my piano lesson |

Example: A: What are you <u>training</u> for?
B: I'm <u>training</u> for <u>the race</u>.

Write

Read the question. Write your response in your notebook.

What is something you practice, train, rehearse, or study for? Write two or three sentences about it.

Make Connections

Copy the sentences into your notebook and complete them.

play in a concert

get good grades

win a ribbon

act in a play

1. I like to run. I train after school every day.
   I want to _____ in a race this year.

2. I'm in the school play this year. It's my first time
   to _____ . It's fun!

3. I practice the piano every day. Soon I can _____!

4. I ask a lot of questions in class, so I learn a lot.
   I study hard, too, so I usually _____.

What about you?

Talk with a partner about some of the challenges you
have at school and at home. How do you meet these
challenges? Who can help you?

Kids' Stories from around the World

Audio

Korea

India

Ethiopia

Abebe

I live in Ethiopia. I want to be a good runner. Each morning, I train before I go to school. Each afternoon, I train after school. Then I go home and do my homework. If I train hard, I can be a great runner.

Krishna

I live in India. Every day after school, I do my homework. Then I go to see my chess coach. I play chess with her for two hours. If I work hard, I can enter a chess contest.

Costa Rica

Pedro

In Costa Rica, we have many rain forests. Our rain forests are in danger. Some people want to cut down the trees. Then the animals will not have homes. My parents and I try to help. We teach people about the animals in the rain forest.

Cho

I practice *tae kwon do* three times a week. *Tae kwon do* is a martial art from Korea. It is hard, but I like it. We learn to kick. We learn to move fast. If I practice, I can become strong.

What about you?

1. What do you challenge yourself to do, either every day or a few times a week?

2. How did you meet a big challenge in your life? Share your story.

Reading 1

Prepare to Read

What You Will Learn

Reading

- Vocabulary building: *Context, phonics*

- Reading strategy: *Identify events in a plot*

- Text type: *Literature (play)*

Grammar

Possessive nouns and pronouns

Writing

Write a plot summary

These words will help you understand the reading.

Key Words

dinner
well
roars
reflection

Key Words

In *The Rabbit and the Lion,* a smart rabbit plays a trick on a proud lion.

Words in Context

1 All around the world, people eat different foods for dinner.

2 In some places, people cannot get water in their houses. They go to a well to get water. A well is a deep hole in the ground. The hole goes down to where there is water.

3 Different animals make different noises. A duck quacks. A horse neighs. A dog barks. A lion roars!

4 The reflection in this lake is very clear. You can see the mountains, trees, and clouds in the water.

Make flashcards to help you memorize the words.

- Write a key word on the front.
- On the back, draw a picture of the word.

Speaking Skills

If you don't know the exact English word to use, explain your idea with words you know.

Make Connections

In this play, animals talk and act like people. If you could be an animal, what animal would you be? Why? Discuss.

41

These words will help you talk about the reading.

Academic Words

focus
pay attention to

identify
tell what something is

Academic Words

Words in Context

When I take a test, I **focus** on the easy questions first.

My dad can **identify** different kinds of airplanes by their shape.

Practice

Write the sentences in your notebook. Choose an academic word to complete each sentence.

1. I can _____ different kinds of birds by the colors of their feathers.

2. Hanna can't watch TV now. She has to _____ on her homework.

Apply

Ask and answer with a partner.

1. Can you **focus** on your homework and listen to music at the same time?

2. How can you **identify** something that is cooking in the kitchen before you see it?

WB
42

Phonics

Long Vowel Pairs

Long vowel sounds can be spelled with two vowels together making a pair. Listen. Then read each word aloud.

Long *o* Pairs		Long *u* Pairs	
road	foe	blue	fruit

Rule

When two vowels are together, the first vowel says its name.
- The letters *oa* or *oe* usually have the long *o* sound.
- The letters *ue* or *ui* usually have the long *u* sound.

Practice

Work with a partner. Take turns sounding out the words in the box.

clue	toad	woe	foam	fruit	suit
doe	true	loan	toe	cue	soak

- Write a list of the words that have the long o sound.
- Write a list of the words that have the long u sound.

43

LITERATURE
Play

More About

Sometimes, a character meets a challenge with quick thinking. How can thinking be helpful?

 Listen to the Audio.
Listen for the general meaning. Use the pictures to help you understand the selection.

Reading Strategy

Identify Events in a Plot

As you read, think about the important events.

- Lion catches Rabbit.
- Rabbit tries to save himself. How?

Listen as your teacher models the reading strategy.

The Rabbit and the Lion

by Ed Vuong
illustrated by Tim Haggerty

Characters
Narrator
Rabbit
Lion

characters people or animals in a play or story
narrator person who tells a story

Narrator: Rabbit is smart. But one night his **foe**, Lion, catches him.

Rabbit: Help!

Lion: I have you now, Rabbit! I am going to eat you for dinner!

Rabbit: I am too small. You need a big animal to eat.

Lion: Yes. But you are just the right size for a **snack**.

Rabbit: Who are you to go around eating rabbits?

Lion: I am king of this forest!

Rabbit: Look at the lion in the well. He says he is king!

---

foe enemy
snack small bit of food to eat

Before You Go On How does Rabbit change Lion's **focus** so he is thinking about himself and not about Rabbit?

Narrator: Lion looks into the well. He sees a lion in the water.

Rabbit: Ha! Ha! He thinks his own reflection is another lion!

Narrator: Lion roars at his own reflection in the water in the well.

Lion: You are a **fake**! I AM KING OF THIS FOREST!

Narrator: But a strange voice comes back out of the well.

Voice: I AM KING OF THIS FOREST!

Rabbit: Hee! Hee! It is this silly king's own voice. It is an **echo**.

---

fake   someone who is not what they seem to be
echo   sound you hear again

Reading Skill

Ask your classmates or your teacher if you do not understand a word, phrase, or language structure.

Lion:	Fake! You will be sorry for this!
Narrator:	Lion jumps into the well. But the other lion is gone!
Lion:	Where are you? Come out!
Rabbit:	I guess I am king of this forest tonight. See you tomorrow, Lion.

44–46

Reading Strategy

Identify Events in a Plot

- What does Rabbit tell Lion?

- What does Lion do?

- How did **identifying** the events help you see how Rabbit saves himself?

Think It Over

1. **Recall** What does Lion want to do to Rabbit?

2. **Comprehend** Lion cannot **identify** himself in his reflection. Who does he think is in the well?

3. **Analyze** What happens when Lion roars into the well? Why does this make him more angry?

Learning Strategies

Events in a Plot

Events are the things that happen in a play. The events make up the plot. The **plot** is the main story of a play.

Practice

Read these lines from the play. Tell who says each line. Then tell which events show how Rabbit tricks Lion.

1. Help!
2. But you are just the right size for a snack.
3. I am king of this forest!
4. Look at the lion in the well. He says he is king!
5. Ha! Ha! He thinks his own reflection is another lion!
6. Lion jumps into the well.

Use a Sequence Chart

In this play, the events happen in a certain order. One event makes the next one happen.

Copy the Sequence Chart. Answer the questions to complete it.

1. Which is the best sentence for Number 3 in the chart?
   a. Lion jumps into the well.
   b. Rabbit thinks the reflection in the well is another lion.
   c. Lion thinks his reflection in the well is another lion.

2. Which is the best sentence for Number 6 in the chart?
   a. Lion jumps into the well to fight his reflection.
   b. Rabbit says that Lion is king of this forest.
   c. Lion says that Rabbit is king of this forest.

1	Lion catches Rabbit. Lion says that he is going to eat Rabbit.
2	Rabbit says there is another lion in the well.
3	
4	Lion roars and shouts at the reflection in the well.
5	An echo from the well comes back out at Lion.
6	

Retell the play to a partner.
Refer to the pictures as you speak.

47

Extension

Utilize Work with a partner. Make up a skit. Show how the characters solve a problem. As you work together, listen to each other's ideas. Present your skit to the class.

Grammar

Possessive Nouns and Pronouns

A **pronoun** takes the place of a noun.

Singular Pronouns		Plural Pronouns
I/me	→	we/us
you	→	you
he, she, it/him, her, it	→	they/them

A pronoun must match the noun it replaces. This noun is called the **antecedent**. For a female, the pronoun is *she* or *her*. For a male, it is *he* or *him*. For a plural, it is *they* or *them*.

> **Lion** wants dinner. **He** wants dinner.
> Rabbit tricks **Lion**. Rabbit tricks **him**.
> **Ana** likes **stories**. **She** reads **them** to the class.

Use **possessive pronouns** or **possessive nouns** (*'s*) to show ownership or belonging. For plural nouns ending in *-s*, just use an apostrophe after the *-s*.

Possessive Pronouns	Possessive Nouns
my/our	the **lion's** reflection
your	the **king's** voice
his/her/its/their	the **students'** questions

To make a **question**, use *whose* before the noun.

> **Whose** pencil is this? → This is **my** pencil.

Practice

Choose the correct pronoun. Write the sentences.

Example: A soccer game is on TV. Let's watch (it, them).

A soccer game is on TV. Let's watch it.

1. Do you like dogs? I like (him, them).

2. My sister is not here. (She, He) is absent.

3. Javier is my brother. (He, She) is nice.

4. I love my cats. (They, Them) are sweet.

5. Where are my sisters? Do you see (her, them)?

Apply

Work with a partner. Ask and answer the questions.
Use possessive nouns and pronouns in your answers.

Example: A: Whose pen is this?

B: This is my pen.

- Whose pen is this?
- Whose notebook is that?
- Whose pencils are those?
- Whose books are those?
- Whose backpack is that?
- Whose eraser is that?
- Whose desk is that over there?
- Whose picture is that on the wall?

48

Grammar Check ✓

Name some **possessive pronouns.**

Writing

Write a Plot Summary

One way to write about a story is to summarize the plot. This means you tell the main ideas in the story.

Writing Prompt

Write a paragraph summarizing the plot of a story. Tell the events in the correct order. Include details about what the characters say and do. Be sure to use possessive nouns and pronouns correctly.

❶ Prewrite

Choose a story to summarize. Who are the characters? What are the events that happen? List your ideas in a Sequence Chart.

A student named Bruno listed his ideas like this:

THE RABBIT AND THE LION

> Lion catches Rabbit. He wants to eat Rabbit.

> Rabbit tricks Lion. Lion thinks there is another lion in the well.

> Lion jumps into the well. Rabbit is safe.

❷ Draft

Use your Sequence Chart to help you write a first draft.

- Keep in mind your purpose—to write a plot summary.
- Include the events of the story in the correct order.

❸ Revise

Reread your draft. Look for places where it needs improvement. Use the Writing Checklist to help you find problems. Then revise your draft.

❹ Edit

Check your work for errors. Use the Peer Review Checklist on page 402.

❺ Publish

Make a clean copy of your final draft. Share it with the class. Save your work. You will need it for the Writing Workshop.

Here is Bruno's plot summary:

Bruno Silva

"The Rabbit and the Lion"
by Ed Vuong

One night, Lion catches Rabbit. Lion wants to eat Rabbit, but Rabbit tricks Lion. He tells Lion to look in the well. Lion sees another lion in the well. It is lion's reflection. Lion shouts, "I am the king of the forest." He hears his echo: "I am the king of the forest." Lion is angry. He jumps into the well. Now Rabbit is safe.

Writing Checklist

Ideas

✓ I included all the events in the correct order.

✓ I expressed my ideas clearly.

Conventions

✓ I used possessive pronouns correctly.

✓ I used possessive nouns ('s) correctly.

WB 49–50

What You Will Learn

Reading

- Vocabulary building: *Context, word study*

- Reading strategy: *Visualize*

- Text type: *Literature (fable)*

Grammar
Simple past: regular verbs

Writing
Retell a familiar story

These words will help you understand the reading.

Key Words

clouds
stronger
spiders
webs
brighter

Key Words

In *The Contest,* North Wind and Sun find out who is stronger.

Words in Context

1 Some clouds are puffy and light. Some clouds are dark and heavy. Which ones do you think bring rain?

2 Which bridge is stronger?

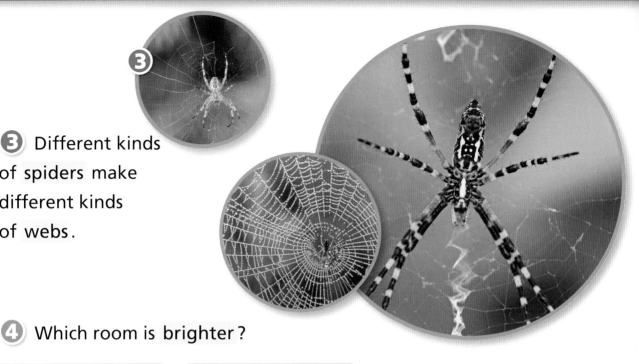

③ Different kinds of spiders make different kinds of webs.

④ Which room is brighter?

 **Practice**

Make flashcards to help you memorize the words.

- Write a key word on the front.
- On the back, write the meaning.

Make Connections

In this story, one character wants to win. Do you think winning is important? Why or why not? Discuss.

Speaking Skills

When you're not sure what word or phrase to use, use gestures to express your idea.

WB

51

These words will help you talk about the reading.

Academic Words

affect
produce a change

attitude
way of thinking

Academic Words

Words in Context

The weather did not **affect** our trip. We were going no matter what.

Even though this class is difficult, we like it. We have a positive **attitude** about this class.

Practice

Write the sentences in your notebook. Choose an academic word to complete each sentence.

1. Even when he loses, he doesn't get angry. He has a positive _____ about sports.

2. Don't look directly at the sun. It will _____ your eyes badly.

Apply

Ask and answer with a partner.

1. How does rain **affect** the way you feel?

2. How can a good **attitude** help you?

WB
52

Word Study

Prefixes and Suffixes

A **prefix** is a word part added to the beginning of a word.

A **suffix** is a word part added to the end of a word.

Rule

Look for this pattern in English: when you add a prefix or suffix to a word, it changes the word's meaning. For example:

The prefix *dis* means **not**. So *disagree* means **not agree**.

The suffix *less* means **without**. So *restless* means **without rest**.

Practice

Read the sentences with a partner. Take turns.

• Tell the meaning of each word with the prefix *dis*.

• Tell the meaning of each word with the suffix *less*.

1. The sun is disappearing behind the clouds.

2. My sister and I disagree.

3. Mr. Ashton dislikes loud music.

4. At first the North Wind is thoughtless.

5. It's a beautiful, cloudless day.

53

LITERATURE
Fable

More About

Do you always need to be strong to meet a challenge?

Audio Listen to the Audio.
Listen for the general meaning. Use the pictures to help you understand the selection.

Reading Strategy

Visualize

As you read, try to make pictures in your head.

- Where are the characters?
- What do they look like?
- What are they doing?

Listen as your teacher models the reading strategy.

The Contest

by Matt Aun
illustrated by Stephen Alcorn

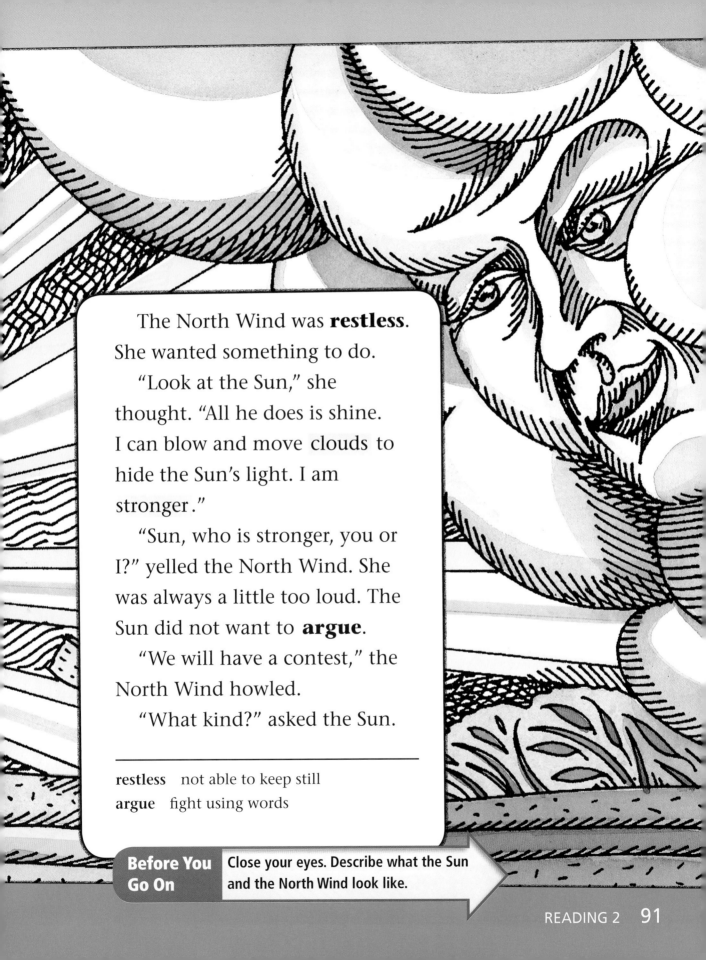

The North Wind was **restless**. She wanted something to do.

"Look at the Sun," she thought. "All he does is shine. I can blow and move clouds to hide the Sun's light. I am stronger."

"Sun, who is stronger, you or I?" yelled the North Wind. She was always a little too loud. The Sun did not want to **argue**.

"We will have a contest," the North Wind howled.

"What kind?" asked the Sun.

---

restless   not able to keep still
argue   fight using words

Before You Go On | Close your eyes. Describe what the Sun and the North Wind look like.

The North Wind saw a woman walking on Earth. She wore a hat.

"Make that woman take off her hat," ordered the North Wind.

"You go first," said the Sun. The North Wind laughed. She thought the contest would be easy. She took a deep breath and blew. She pushed clouds to cover the Sun. She blew so hard the trees were bending. The spiders held tight to their webs.

But the woman walked on. She held on to her hat.

The North Wind took another breath and then she blew very hard. She blew leaves from the trees. She pushed flying birds from the sky. They hid in their nests. The North Wind threw spiders to the ground. She sent their webs flying away.

In the strong wind, it was hard for the woman to stay on her feet. But she never let go of her hat. She held it on her head with both hands.

Before You Go On What does the North Wind do to try and make the woman take off her hat?

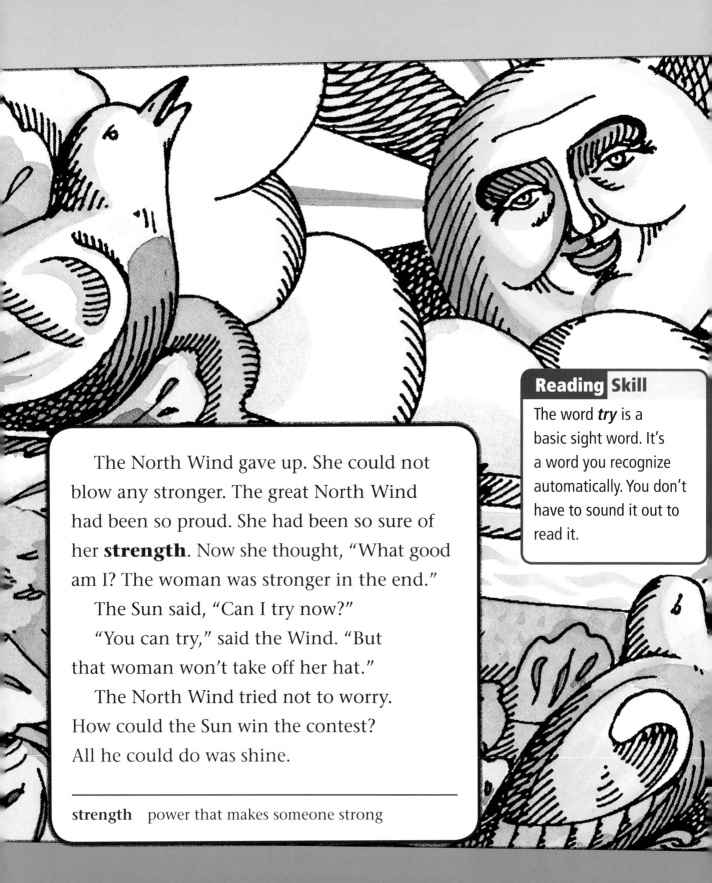

The North Wind gave up. She could not blow any stronger. The great North Wind had been so proud. She had been so sure of her **strength**. Now she thought, "What good am I? The woman was stronger in the end."

The Sun said, "Can I try now?"

"You can try," said the Wind. "But that woman won't take off her hat."

The North Wind tried not to worry. How could the Sun win the contest? All he could do was shine.

---

strength   power that makes someone strong

Reading Skill

The word *try* is a basic sight word. It's a word you recognize automatically. You don't have to sound it out to read it.

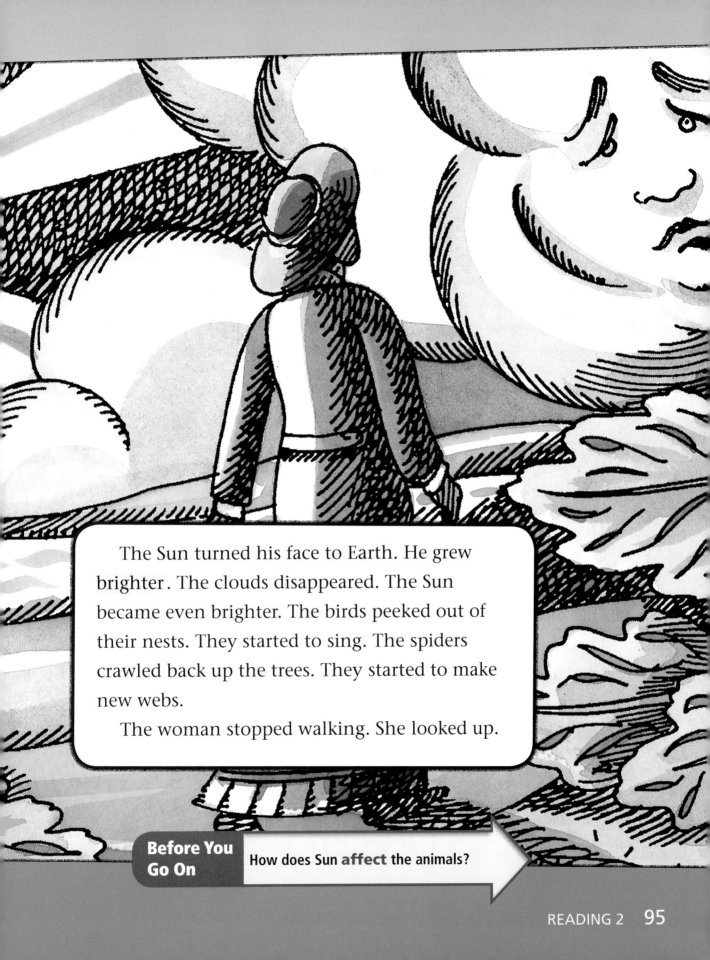

The Sun turned his face to Earth. He grew brighter. The clouds disappeared. The Sun became even brighter. The birds peeked out of their nests. They started to sing. The spiders crawled back up the trees. They started to make new webs.

The woman stopped walking. She looked up.

Before You Go On How does Sun **affect** the animals?

The Sun looked down at the woman and shone even brighter.

"It's getting very hot," said the woman. She took off her hat and sat down under a tree.

The Wind said, "You win. You are stronger."

"You are strong in some ways," said the Sun. "I am strong in others. Why does it matter? Each of us does our job."

The North Wind looked at the woman. The North Wind blew a tiny puff of air.

The woman smiled. She thought, "It's nice to have a cool **breeze** on such a hot day."

The North Wind smiled and thought, "Each of us does do our job."

---

breeze   light wind

WB
54–56

Reading Strategy

Visualize

- Where are the Sun and North Wind?

- What do the Sun and North Wind look like?

- How did visualizing help you understand the story?

Think It Over

1. **Recall**   What is the contest?

2. **Comprehend**   Before the contest, what is North Wind's **attitude**?

3. **Analyze**   After the contest, how does North Wind show that she has a new attitude?

Learning Strategies

Visualizing

As you read, you can **visualize**, or make pictures in your head. You may make pictures of where the characters are. You may make pictures of what the characters look like. You may picture what is happening in the story.

Practice

Read each sentence. Describe the pictures you make in your mind. Choose one sentence and draw it.

1. The North Wind was restless. She wanted something to do.

2. The Sun turned his face to Earth. He grew brighter.

3. In the strong wind, it was hard for the woman to stay on her feet.

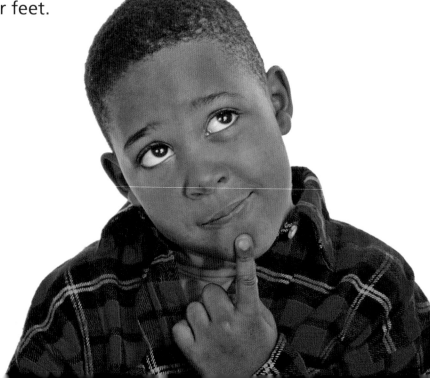

Use a Compare and Contrast Chart

When you **compare,** you look for things that are the same. When you **contrast,** you look for things that are different. You can compare and contrast the different types of writing, or **genres** in this unit.

Copy the chart. List each of the statements below in the correct column. Some of the genres may have more than one statement.

Story	Play	Poem

- has events in a plot
- uses rhyme
- lists the name of the characters
- tells about conflicts

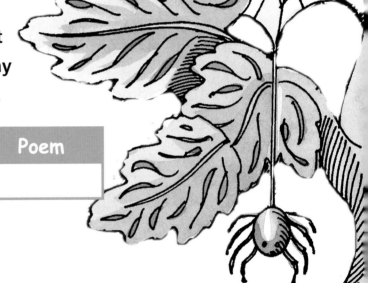

Retell the fable to a partner. Refer to the pictures as you speak.

Extension

Utilize   Work in a group of four to act out *The Contest* as a play. One person is the director. The actors should follow the director's instructions. Present your play to the class.

Grammar

Simple Past: Regular Verbs

Verbs in the **simple past** tell what happened before now.
A simple past verb has the same form for all subjects.

I **walk** away.	⟶	I **walked** away.
The woman **walks** away.	⟶	The woman **walked** away.

Make the simple past of regular verbs by adding -ed.

Add **-d** to verbs ending in -e.	live ⟶ lived
Change the **y** to **i** and add -ed to verbs ending in a consonant and -y.	try ⟶ tried
Add **-ed** to verbs ending in a vowel and **-y.**	stay ⟶ stayed
Double the consonant and add **-ed** for verbs with a stressed CVC ending.	occur ⟶ occurred

To make **negative sentences** in the past tense, add *did not* before the plain form of the verb.

Positive	Negative
We **laughed**. ⟶	We **did not laugh**.

did not = **didn't**

To make **questions** in the past tense, use *did* before the subject.

Did you stay?	Yes, I **did**.
	Yes, I **stayed**.

Practice

Use the past tense form of the verb in parentheses. Write the sentences.

Example: The Sun <u>asked</u> a question. (ask)

1. The North Wind ____ the clouds around. (push)

2. The Sun ____ down. (look)

3. The heat ____ everyone. (**affect**)

4. The spiders ____ back to their webs. (crawl)

5. The Wind ____ something important. (learn)

Apply

Work with a partner. Ask and answer the questions about this week. Use simple past regular verbs in your answers.

Example: A: Did you call a friend this week?
              B: Yes, I called a friend.

- Did you call a friend this week?
- Did a friend visit you at home?
- Did you watch television?
- Did you help your family?
- Did you study every day?
- Did you try something new?

58

Grammar Check ✓

Name the **past tense** of three regular verbs.

Retell a Familiar Story

One way to write a narrative essay is to retell a familiar story in your own words.

Writing Prompt

Write a paragraph retelling a story you like. Use your own words. Describe what the characters say and do. Be sure to use the simple past correctly.

❶ Prewrite   G.O. 149

Choose a story to retell. Who are the characters? What are the events that happen? List your ideas in a T-Chart.

A student named Carmen listed her ideas like this:

HARE AND THE TORTOISE	
Beginning	Hare and Tortoise agreed to race.
Middle	Hare raced quickly at first, then stopped and rested. Tortoise walked slowly and steadily.
End	Hare hurried to the finish line. Tortoise was already there.

❷ Draft

Use your T-Chart to help you write a draft.

• Keep in mind your purpose—to retell a familiar story.

• Include the beginning, the middle, and the end of the story.

❸ Revise

Read your draft. Look for places where the writing needs improvement. Use the Writing Checklist to help you find problems. Then revise your draft.

❹ Edit

Check your work for errors. Use the Peer Review Checklist on page 402.

❺ Publish

Make a clean copy of your final draft. Share it with the class. Save your work. You will need it for the Writing Workshop.

Here is Carmen's retelling of the story:

Carmen Delgado

Hare and Tortoise

Hare laughed at slow Tortoise. "I can beat you in a race," he said. Tortoise answered, "Let's race and see." They started the race. Hare hopped away. He chased butterflies. Then he stopped under a tree and rested. Tortoise just walked and walked. Later, Hare opened his eyes. "Oh, no. I have to hurry." When Hare arrived at the finish line, Tortoise was already there.

59–60

What You Will Learn

Reading

- Vocabulary building: *Context, phonics*

- Reading strategy: *Identify fact and opinion*

- Text type: *Informational text (social studies)*

Grammar
Simple past: *be* verbs

Writing
Write a journal entry about your day

These words will help you understand the reading.

Key Words

neighborhood
garden
seeds
soil
plants

Key Words

Sharing a Garden is about a neighborhood that works together to create a community garden.

Words in Context

In our neighborhood, we have a community garden. People grow flowers there. They grow vegetables, too.

First, we put seeds in the rich, dark soil, or ground. Then seeds grow into plants. We water the plants. They grow and grow.

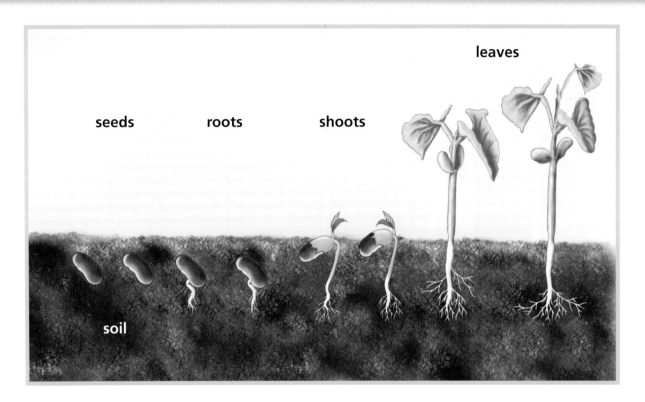

seeds   roots   shoots   leaves

soil

Practice

Draw a picture of a neighborhood garden in your notebook. Label the picture using sentences that contain the key words.

Make Connections

Have you ever planted a seed for a flower or plant? How well did it grow? Would you like to work in a neighborhood garden? After you discuss these questions, write your responses in your notebook.

61

These words will help you talk about the reading.

Academic Words

interact
communicate

outcome
result

Academic Words

Words in Context

Students talk and **interact** with each other when they do a project together.

Our team played well the whole game. The **outcome** was that we won!

Practice

Write the sentences in your notebook. Choose an academic word to complete each sentence.

1. During lunch we can _____ with kids from other grades.

2. When I study hard, the _____ is usually good.

Apply

Ask and answer with a partner.

1. What are some ways a child or an adult can **interact** with a baby?

2. What was the **outcome** of the last game you played?

WB
62

Phonics

More Long Vowel Pairs

Long vowel pairs can make the long *a*, long *e*, or long *i* sounds. Listen. Then read each word aloud.

Long *a* Pairs		Long *e* Pairs		Long *i* Pair
day	rain	keep	neat	pie

Rule

When two vowels are together, the first vowel says its name.

- The letters *ai* or *ay* usually have the long *a* sound.
- The letters *ee* or *ea* usually have the long *e* sound.
- The letters *ie* usually have the long *i* sound.

Practice

Work with a partner. Take turns. Listen for words that have long vowel sounds.

Long *a*	Long *e*	Long *i*

- Copy the chart.
- Find and list the words with long vowel pairs.

1. Is that a bird in the tree?
2. What a long tail it has!
3. Pass the treat this way.
4. Let's have some pie.

63

More About

What are some challenges in starting a community garden?

Listen to the Audio. Listen for the general meaning. Use the pictures to help you understand the selection.

Reading Strategy

Identify Fact and Opinion

A fact is something that is real or true. An opinion is what someone thinks.

- Identify statements in this reading that are facts. If it is a fact, you can prove it is true.

- Identify statements in this reading that are opinions. If it is an opinion, you cannot prove it is true or false.

Listen as your teacher models the reading strategy.

Sharing a Garden

by Terry Miller Shannon

A community garden is a garden grown by a group of people. Every neighborhood could benefit from a community garden.

Why do people want a community garden? Some people want a garden, but they do not have a place to put one. Other people do not want to work on a garden alone. They want to share a garden.

Community gardens can help **improve** people's lives. Gardeners may become healthier by eating fresh vegetables. They can enjoy lots of fresh air and exercise, too.

Gardens make neighborhoods look more beautiful. Sometimes city people don't have a chance to enjoy nature. With a community garden, they can see something beautiful every day.

---

improve   make better

Fresh vegetables grown in a garden make healthy food choices.

Before You Go On   What are some reasons people start community gardens?

A community garden takes work. Here is the story of how one neighborhood planned their garden.

Before any seeds were planted, a group of neighbors got together. They made a list of everything that had to be done. They decided where to put the garden. They decided what kind of garden it would be. They even decided on a name for the garden!

Fortunately, the people in the planning group didn't have to do everything themselves. They were able to give some of these jobs to different people.

---

fortunately   luckily

This group is planning their community garden.

Next, the gardeners prepared the soil. They dug the soil to remove the weeds. Some gardeners worked by hand, and some gardeners worked with a machine.

When the soil was ready, the gardeners started to plant. They **sowed** seeds and placed small plants in the garden.

They cared for their garden together for **several** weeks. Day by day, under the bright sun, the group shared **chores**. Some pulled weeds. Others watered the plants.

---

sow   plant

several   some

chores   jobs that must be done regularly

This girl is getting ready to plant a garden.

Before You Go On   What was the **outcome** of preparing the soil?

Finally, it was time to pick the beans, corn, greens, and other fresh **produce**. They divided the food. They took it home to enjoy with their family and friends.

The gardeners were proud of the work they contributed. "Sometimes the work was hard," said one gardener. "But the **reward** was good food, and the chance to get to know my neighbors."

---

produce   fruits and vegetables
reward   good thing you receive

People work together in a shared community garden.

Dear Neighbors,

We were wondering if you would like to start a garden with your neighbors. Friends who were part of a shared garden say it was a wonderful adventure! In our garden, we will not grow just plants. We will grow a strong friendship between gardeners. This will make our community stronger.

As we dig, weed, and plant, we will discover other benefits. A garden filled with green plants will make our neighborhood more beautiful. It will make us healthier, too. Doctors say we need to eat more vegetables and get more exercise. Our families would eat better, thanks to lots of tasty produce. Gardening is good exercise, too.

Neighbors, please join us in our new adventure!

Many thanks,
Ann and Dan Jones

WB
64–66

Reading Strategy

Fact and Opinion

- Which statements were facts that can be proved?
- Which statements were opinions?

Think It Over

1. **Recall** What decisions did the neighbors make before they started on the garden?

2. **Comprehend** What are some jobs in a community garden?

3. **Analyze** How can a community garden make people **interact**?

Learning Strategies

Identify Fact and Opinion

A **fact** is something that can be proved. An **opinion** is what someone thinks.

- Statements of facts are points that are true. They can be proven.

- Statements of opinion are points that someone makes based on what they believe.

Practice

Tell whether the statements below are fact or opinion. Look carefully for clue words that help you decide. Remember that often an opinion is how someone feels, but can not be proven.

1. A community garden is one garden grown by a group of people.
2. These wonderful gardens are an important part of the neighborhood.
3. Working together in a community garden is a good way for neighbors to become friends.
4. The garden must get sunlight. The sunlight helps the plants to grow.
5. Gardens must be watered on days it doesn't rain.

Use an Idea Web

An Idea Web can help you see how different ideas in a story are connected.

Copy this Idea Web. Reread *Sharing a Garden.*
Then write down facts and opinions about a community
garden that you learned.

- Share your work with a partner.

- Discuss reasons why planting a community garden is a good thing for a neighborhood.

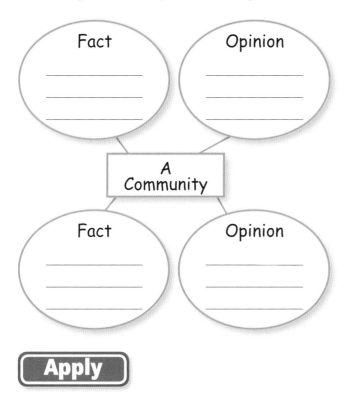

Fact

Opinion

A Community

Fact

Opinion

67

Apply

Summarize the selection. Use some of the key words as you speak.

Extension

Utilize Think of a project you could start in your community, such as a community library, or a community recycling center. Write a letter inviting your neighbors to join your project. Display your letter in the classroom.

Grammar

Simple Past: *be* Verbs

Use the **simple past** of *be* to talk about events that started and finished in the past.

The soil is ready. ⟶	The soil was ready.
They are neighbors. ⟶	They were neighbors.

Simple past *be* verbs must agree with the subject.

Subject	Present	Past
I	am	was
He/She/It	is	was
You/They/We	are	were

You can use **contractions** of *be* verbs in negative sentences.

Our garden wasn't big.
The chores weren't easy.

was not = **wasn't**
were not = **weren't**

To ask questions, put the *be* verbs before the **subject**.

Was the **work** hard?
Yes, it was. / No, it wasn't.
Were the **seeds** fresh?
Yes, they were. / No, they weren't.

Practice

Change each *be* verb to its simple past form.
Write the sentences.

Example: Each community garden is different.

Each community garden was different.

1. My neighbors are at the meeting.

2. The work is interesting.

3. Their jobs are different every day.

4. The squash plants are really big.

5. Is it difficult to grow peas?

Apply

Work with a partner. Ask and answer questions about the school you went to last year. Use simple past *be* verbs in your answers.

Example: A: Were you in this school last year?

B: Yes, I was.

- Were you in this school last year?
- Who was your teacher?
- What was the best thing about your class?
- Who were some of your friends?
- What was your favorite subject?
- Were there animals or pets in your class?

W B
68

Grammar Check ✓

Write a question using a **simple past *be* verb.**

Writing

Write a Journal Entry about Your Day

Ongoing Writing Skills Practice

A journal entry is another type of narrative essay.

Writing Prompt

Write a paragraph telling about something that happened to you. Say how you felt. Be sure to use the simple past of *be* correctly.

❶ Prewrite   G.O. 152

Think about a day in the past. What did you do? Who did you see? List everything in a Three-Column Chart.

A student named Emily listed her ideas like this:

FACTS	SENSORY DETAILS	EMOTIONS
My teacher put a test on my desk. →	My brain was frozen. →	I was nervous.
My teacher asked, "Are you OK?" →	I couldn't move. →	I was scared.
My teacher smiled. →	My body relaxed. →	I felt better.

❷ Draft

Use your Three-Column Chart to help you write a first draft.

• Keep in mind your purpose—to write a journal entry.

• Write about how you felt and what you remember.

❸ Revise

Reread your draft. Look for places where it needs improvement. Use the Writing Checklist to help you find problems. Then revise your draft.

❹ Edit

Check your work for errors. Use the Peer Review Checklist on page 402.

❺ Publish

Make a clean copy of your final draft. Share it with the class. Save your work. You will need it for the Writing Workshop.

Here is Emily's journal entry:

Writing Checklist

Ideas

✓ I included the events in the correct order.

✓ I expressed my ideas clearly.

Voice

✓ I talked about how I felt.

Conventions

✓ I used verbs in the simple past tense correctly.

✓ I used punctuation and quotation marks correctly.

> Wednesday, January 15th
>
> I wasn't in school yesterday. This morning, my teacher put a math test on my desk. Suddenly I was nervous. I couldn't think. My brain was frozen. My teacher asked, "Are you OK?" But I couldn't move. I was scared. Then my teacher smiled. She said, "You weren't here yesterday. Don't worry. I'll help you." After that, my whole body relaxed. I felt much better.

69–70

Apply and Extend

Link the Readings

Copy the chart into your notebook. Read the words in the top row.

- For *The Rabbit and the Lion*, put an X under the words that remind you of the text.

- Repeat the same activity for the other readings.

	Informational text	Literature	Working together	Competition
The Rabbit and the Lion				
The Contest				
Sharing a Garden				

Discussion

1. In *The Rabbit and the Lion*, what is surprising about the **outcome** of the story?

2. Compare and contrast Rabbit with the Sun. How do their **attitudes** help them meet their challenges?

3. What are the rewards of working in a community garden?

THE BIG QUESTION All of us have challenges at times. How can people meet challenges?

> **Listening Skills**
>
> When you are not sure what word or phrase to use, you can use gestures to express your ideas.

Projects

Your teacher will help you choose one of these projects.

Written	Oral	Visual/Active
Email	**Talk and Help**	**What If Book**
Write an email to a friend or relative. Tell that person about a problem you faced and how how you solved the problem.	Give an informal talk to children in first grade. Tell them about challenges you had when you were little and how you met them.	Create a picture book. Show ways to solve problems. For example, show a boy raising his hand to ask a question.
T-Chart	**Act It Out**	**Matching Game**
Create a T-Chart for the selections in this unit. Use **Problem** and **Solution** as the headings.	Work with a partner. Think of a problem to solve. Act out a scene about the problem, and then show the solution.	Write a problem on five cards. Write a solution on five other cards. Have a partner try to match them.

 For more projects visit
LongmanCornerstone.com

Further Reading

The Velveteen Rabbit®, Margery Williams
This Penguin Young Reader® is an adaptation of the classic story about a stuffed toy rabbit. When his owner grows up, the toy rabbit joins the real rabbits.

The Dot, Peter H. Reynolds
In art class, Vashti cannot think of what to draw. Vashti's teacher challenges her to "just make a mark." Vashti's simple dot leads her to a new level of confidence and creativity.

71–72

Listening and Speaking Workshop

Perform a Skit

You are going to write and perform a skit. Then you will listen as your classmates perform a skit, too.

❶ Prepare

A. Find two partners. Choose a scene from one of the readings. Then act it out as a skit.

B. Study your scene and decide where it begins and ends. Who is going to play each part? Now write your skit. Discuss and find props to use in your skit. As you work together, listen to each other's ideas and work cooperatively.

	The Contest
North Wind:	Sun, who is stronger, you or I? We will have a contest.
Sun:	What kind?
North Wind:	Make that woman take off her hat.
Sun:	You go first.
Woman:	Oh, it's windy!

❷ Practice

Practice your skit with your props. Act it out in front of your family or friends. If possible, record your skit. Then listen to it. How do you and your partners sound? Record it again and try to improve.

❸ Present

As you speak, do the following:

- Don't be nervous. Have fun.
- Don't read your skit—act it out.
- Pay attention to your partners, so you know when to say your lines.

As you listen, do the following:

- Watch the actions of the actors.
- Pay close attention. Your teacher will ask you questions after the skit.

❹ Evaluate

After you speak, answer these questions:

✓ Did you act out your skit?

✓ Did you use props?

After you listen, answer these questions:

✓ Did you watch the actions of the actors?

✓ How did the actions help you understand?

✓ Was the skit formal or informal?

Writing Workshop

Write a Story

Writing Prompt

Write a story. Include everything that happened and how you felt.
List the main details in a graphic organizer.

❶ Prewrite G.O. 144

Review the writing you have done in this unit. Now choose
something that happened to you to write about. Include
vivid details. List what happened in a graphic organizer.

A student named Tony listed his ideas like this:

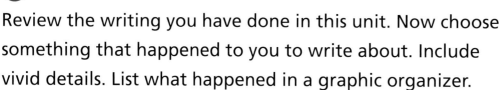

> **Beginning:** I heard a funny noise
> coming from the attic.

> **Middle:** I decided to investigate.
> I went up the attic stairs.

> **End:** It was a mouse caught in a trap.

❷ Draft

Use your chart to help you write a first draft.

- Keep in mind your purpose—to tell a story.
- Include what happened and how you felt.

❸ Revise

Read your draft. Look for places where the writing needs improvement. Use the Writing Checklist to help you find problems. Then revise your draft.

Here is how Tony revised his essay:

Six Traits of Writing Checklist

✓ **Ideas**
Does my story include vivid details?

✓ **Organization**
Does my story have a beginning, middle, and end?

✓ **Voice**
Does my language express my feelings?

✓ **Word Choice**
Did I use specific words?

✓ **Sentence Fluency**
Did I use different kinds of sentences?

✓ **Conventions**
Do pronouns agree with their subjects?

Tony Milanese

The Noise in the Attic

One morning last winter I was lying in bed. It was still dark. I was almost asleep.

Suddenly, I heard something over my head. It was coming from the attic. It sounded like something being dragged ~~draged~~ across the floor. I decided to investigate.

Revised to correct spelling error.

I took my plastic pirate sword for protection. I slowly walked ~~walk~~ up the stairs. I was cold and afraid. Everything was quiet, but I could still hear the dragging noise. Slowly, I opened the door and looked around ~~the door.~~ to see what was there

Revised to correct verb tense.

Revised to make the meaning clearer.

It was a mouse caught by his tail! I let him go outside. I felt very brave!

4 Edit

Check your work for errors. Trade papers with a partner to get feedback. Use the Peer Review Checklist.

5 Publish

Make a clean copy of your final draft. Share it with the class.

73–74

Peer Review Checklist

✓ The events are clear and in an order that makes sense.

✓ The writing is interesting and engaging.

✓ The subjects and verbs agree.

SPELLING TIP

In a one-syllable word, if the word ends in a CVC pattern, double the consonant before you add -ed (drag ⟶ dragged).

Listen to the sentences. Pay attention to the groups of words. Read aloud.

1. A small, smart rabbit can trick a big, strong lion.

2. Everyone can use their strengths to do a good job.

3. If we work together, we can create a beautiful garden.

Work in pairs. Take turns reading aloud the passage below for one minute. Count the number of words you read.

The Contest tells about a competition between the North Wind	10
and the Sun. They see a woman wearing a hat. The North Wind	23
says she will make the lady take off her hat. She blows very hard	37
but the woman holds on to her hat. Then the Sun tries. The Sun	51
grows hotter and brighter. The woman is hot, so she takes off	63
her hat. The North Wind says the Sun is stronger. The Sun says	76
they do their job.	80

With your partner, find the words that slowed you down.

- Practice saying each word and then say the sentence each word is in.
- Then take turns reading the text again. Count the number of words you read.

75

Test Preparation

Taking Tests

You will often take tests that help show what you know. Follow these tips to improve your test-taking skills.

Coaching Corner

Answering Test Questions

- When answering a multiple-choice question, watch out for answer choices that are similar to the correct answer. Think hard about what the question is asking and choose the *best* answer.

- Before you read a selection, preview the questions that go with the selection. Reading the questions first will help you think about the information you need while you read the selection. After you finish reading the selection, read the questions again to help you choose the best answer.

- Before you answer a question based on a picture, read the question carefully. Be sure you understand what the question is asking. Study every part of the picture closely before you choose an answer.

Read the following test sample. Study the tips in the box.

77–78

Read the selection. Then answer the questions.

Prickly Pears

The desert can be a challenging place to live. But the prickly pear cactus is a tough plant! Although the desert only gets a few inches of rain each year, prickly pears can grow to be up to 10 feet tall. Prickly pears have special leaves that store water to keep them healthy in very hot and dry weather. These plants are also covered with sharp, yellow spines to protect them from predators.

1   Which part of a prickly pear cactus helps protect it from animals?

   A leaves

   B pears

   C water

   D spines

Tips

✓ Be careful. All of the answer choices are words from the selection. Only one is correct.

✓ Remember that a fact is always true. An opinion is what someone thinks, but it may not be true.

2   Which of the following sentences is an opinion?

   F The prickly pear cactus is a tough plant!

   G Prickly pears can grow to be 10 feet tall.

   H Prickly pears have special leaves that store water.

   J These plants are covered with sharp, yellow spines.

Animals at Home

What animals change shape as they grow? What do alligators eat? What animals hide right at home? Read on to find out!

Reading

1 | Poem

Animals at Home

2 | Photo Essay

Can You See Them?

3 | Science

How Do They Grow?

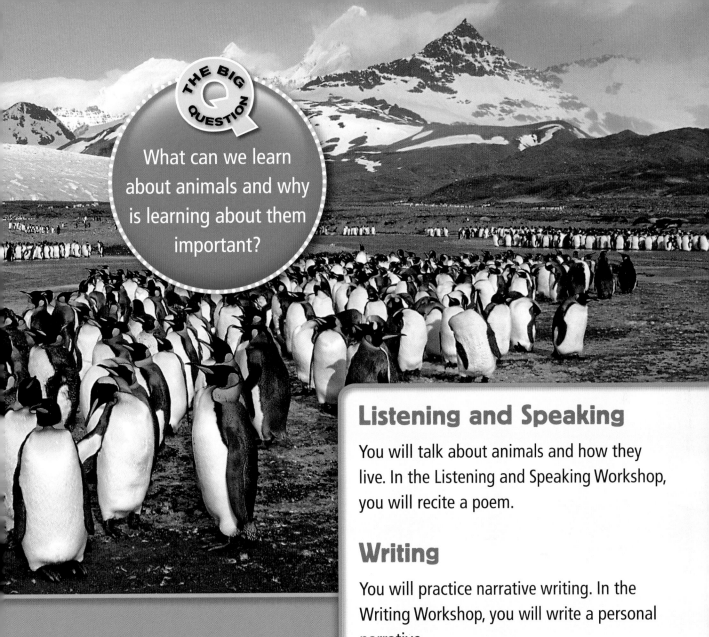

THE BIG QUESTION

What can we learn about animals and why is learning about them important?

Listening and Speaking

You will talk about animals and how they live. In the Listening and Speaking Workshop, you will recite a poem.

Writing

You will practice narrative writing. In the Writing Workshop, you will write a personal narrative.

Quick Write

What is your favorite animal? Write some things you like about this animal.

VIEW AND RESPOND
Talk about the poster for this unit. Then watch and listen to the video and answer the questions at <u>LongmanCornerstone.com</u>.

131

What do you know about animals?

Words to Know

Listen and repeat. Use these words to talk about animals.

 frog

 monkey

 raccoon

 squirrel

 butterfly

 horse

Work with a partner. Look up these words in a dictionary. Then ask and answer questions.

climb	fly	jump	run

Example: A: What can <u>squirrels</u> do?

B: They can <u>climb</u>.

Read the question. Write your response in your notebook.

What animals do you see at the park? What about the zoo?

Make Connections

Copy the sentences into your notebook and complete them.

woods

pond

rain forest

1. A: This animal lives near a ＿＿＿ and likes to jump in the water.

   B: It's a frog.

2. A: This animal lives in the ＿＿＿ . It climbs trees and eats nuts.

   B: It's a squirrel.

3. A: This animal lives in the ＿＿＿ and likes to fly over the trees.

   B: It's a butterfly.

What about you?

Talk with a partner. Choose an animal. Tell your partner where it lives and what it does. Then guess each other's animal.

Kids' Stories from around the World

Audio

Florida, U.S.A.

Senegal

Cassie

I live near the Everglades National Park in Florida. There are lots of insects in the park. That's good, because I like insects. This yellow grasshopper is called an eastern lubber. I see a lot of these grasshoppers in the summer.

Obiajulu

I live near the Niokolo-Koba National Park in Senegal. I can hear the running frog at a pond near my home. Its voice sounds like water dropping in a pail. The running frog does not hop like other frogs. It runs!

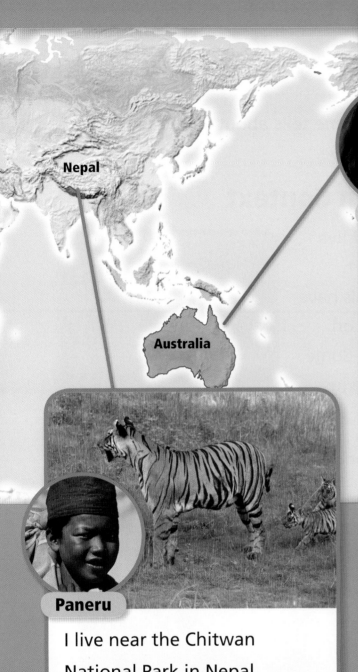

Paige

I live near the Daintree Rain Forest in Australia. I like to watch the butterflies near my home. One of my favorites is the birdwing butterfly. It has yellow wings and a red spot near its head.

Paneru

I live near the Chitwan National Park in Nepal. Tigers live in this park. There are not many tigers left in Nepal. People have hunted them. Today, forest rangers are working hard to protect the tigers.

What about you?

1. What animals do you see where you live?

2. Do you have a story about an animal where you live? Share your story.

What You Will Learn

Reading

- Vocabulary building: *Context, phonics*

- Reading strategy: *Make inferences*

- Text type: *Literature (poem)*

Grammar

Prepositions and prepositional phrases

Writing

Write a poem

These words will help you understand the reading.

Key Words

camels

amazing

habits

caves

plains

Key Words

Animal at Home tells about animals and where they live.

Words in Context

① Camels live in the desert. These camels have two humps on their backs. Some camels have just one hump.

② The flying squirrel is amazing. It does not fly. It jumps and glides through the air.

❸ The children in this family each have different habits. The oldest, David, sings in the shower. Matt runs everywhere. Grace still sucks her thumb. David and Matt hope she will grow out of this habit.

❹ Some bears live in caves. This bear looks out from a cave in the side of a mountain.

❺ Zebras and gazelles live on the wide, flat plains of Africa.

Practice

Add a page to your vocabulary notebook.
- Divide your page into three columns: the new words, their definitions, and drawings of the words (whenever possible).
- Test yourself by covering one of the columns.

Make Connections

Some animals live in caves. Some live on plains. What animals live near you? Where do they live?

These words will help you talk about the reading.

Academic Words
appreciate like or understand the value of something
illustrate show

Academic Words

Words in Context Audio

My mom knows I **appreciate** her cooking because I always say "thank you" after dinner.

The stories **illustrate** interesting places where animals live.

 **Practice**

Write the sentences in your notebook. Choose an academic word to complete each sentence.

1. Your big smile ____ how happy you are.

2. Learning how to play an instrument helps us to ____ music more.

Apply

Ask and answer with a partner.

1. How do you show your friends that you **appreciate** them?

2. What book **illustrates** the kind of story you like to read?

W B

80

Phonics

Consonant Clusters

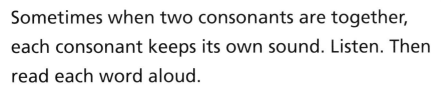

Sometimes when two consonants are together, each consonant keeps its own sound. Listen. Then read each word aloud.

r-blends	*l*-blends	*s*-blends
frog	fly	sky
trees	plains	swim

Rule

Blend the sounds of both letters when a word has

- a consonant followed by the letter *r*
- a consonant followed by the letter *l*
- the letter *s* followed by another consonant

Practice

Work with a partner.

- Choose a word from the chart above to answer each question. Write the answers in your notebook. Use complete sentences.
- Circle each *r*-blend, *s*-blend, or *l*-blend in your answers.

1. Where do monkeys live?
2. Where do zebras live?
3. What do sharks do?
4. What rhymes with *sky*?

81

LITERATURE
Poem

More About

Why should people care where animals live?

Audio **Listen to the Audio.** Listen for the general meaning. Think about the situation or context. Use this to help you understand the poems.

Reading Strategy

Make Inferences

Making inferences helps you figure out information that the author doesn't say directly.

- As you read, think about the different animals.
- Think about why each animal lives where it does.

Listen as your teacher models the reading strategy.

Animals at Home

by Mario Herrera

Animals do amazing things
and have amazing habits.
Some we like to keep at home,
like cats and dogs and rabbits.
Animals live all over the world
in many kinds of homes.
Bats live in caves, monkeys in trees,
and camels in desert zones.

Hippos live their lives in mud
and polar bears in snow.
Zebras live out on the plains
where lions come and go.

Crocodiles live in lakes and rivers,
and fish and snakes do, too.
Whales and sharks and jellyfish
swim in the ocean blue.

Animals share the world with us,
as pets or wild and free.
Animals living in their homes—
what a beautiful sight to see!

Before You Go On   Which line in the poem tells you that the author **appreciates** wild animals?

Little Allie Alligator

by Elizabeth Massie

Little amazing Allie Alligator
Showed bad habits as she
Rested on a log,
In the middle of the morning
In the middle of the fog.
She stretched her legs and
tail out.
She smiled and closed her eyes.
She listened to the river,
To the breeze and buzzing flies.

The fog soon rolled away.
The sun shone bright and hot.
But little amazing Allie Alligator
Stayed right in her spot.

"Come on," said Allie's father.
"It's time for us to eat.
Get down and off that log.
Get up and on your feet!"

But little Allie Alligator
Just lay there on the log
As her father went alone
To find a big and **yummy** frog.
She slept all day and then
she woke,
As hungry as a bear.
Her father laughed and said,
"You won't catch supper
lying there!"

---

yummy   slang word for *delicious*

Tongue Twister:

Grumpy green gators **gobble grubs** in the grass.

Riddles:

What was the alligator doing on the highway?

About two miles an hour.

How many alligators does it take to drive a car?

Three. One to steer. One to push the pedals. And one to yell out the window, "Get out of the way! Don't you know alligators can't drive?"

---

gobble   eat
grubs   larva that look like thick worms

WB
82–84

Reading Strategy

Make Inferences

- Why do you think different kinds of animals have different kinds of homes?

- What can you infer about the crocodiles?

Think It Over

1. **Recall**   What are the two ways animals share the world with us?

2. **Comprehend**   What lines in the poem about Allie Alligator **illustrate** her "bad habits?"

3. **Analyze**   How is the description of animal homes different in the two poems?

Alligators

▲ Eggs in a nest
A mother alligator lays many eggs in a nest.

▲ Going to water
The mother alligator takes the baby alligator to water. Babies know how to swim right away by instinct.

▲ Hatching
A baby alligator hatches. It comes out of its shell.

▲ Free ride
This baby alligator rests on its mother's head.

▲ Food

A grown alligator eats turtles. Alligators like to eat fish, too. An alligator uses its teeth to catch food. It does not chew the food. It swallows the food whole.

▲ Friends

This young alligator shares a log with a painted turtle. But the turtle needs to be careful.

▲ Sunning themselves

Alligators are usually in or near water. Alligators warm themselves in the sun. This one rests on rocks in a swamp.

Activity to Do

These two pages use pictures and captions (words) to tell you about alligators.

• Choose another animal.

• Find pictures of the animal and write captions.

• Post your pictures and captions in your classroom.

Learning Strategies

Inferences

You make **inferences** when you figure out something as you read.

Practice

Make inferences about the poem, *Animals at Home.*

- Read the poem.
- Put together what you know and what you read.

> Animals share the world with us,
>
> as pets or wild and free.
>
> Animals living in their homes —
>
> what a beautiful sight to see!

1. How do pets share the world with us?

2. How do wild animals share the world with us?

3. How are the homes of pets and wild animals different?

Use a KWL Chart

You can use a KWL Chart to make inferences. KWL stands for What You **Know,** What You **Want** to Know, and What You **Learned.**

 G.O. 145

Copy the chart. Answer the questions below. Your answers will help you fill in the chart.

What You Know	What You Want to Know	What You Learned
The poem says "Animals share the world with us."	How do animals and people share the world?	People need to **appreciate** wild animals and where they live.
The poem says that it is "beautiful" to see animals in their homes.	_____ _____ _____ _____	_____ _____ _____ _____

1. What is special about animals' homes? Why is it "beautiful" to see animals where they live?
2. How does the poet feel about animals in their homes?

W B
85

Apply

Summarize the poem *Animals at Home* for a partner. Include inferences you have made about the poem in your summary. Use some of the key words.

Extension

Utilize Work in pairs. Choose an animal. Do research independently on where the animal lives and what it eats. Share your information with your partner. Create a chart together. Share it with the class.

Grammar

Prepositions and Prepositional Phrases

A **preposition of location** is a word that shows where something is.

> Crocodiles live **in** lakes.

A preposition is always followed by a **noun** or **pronoun**. A **prepositional phrase** is a preposition + noun (or pronoun) + any other words that modify the noun.

> We keep dogs **at home.**
> Whales swim **in the ocean blue.**

Review these common prepositions of location and the types of phrases they appear in.

Preposition	Prepositional Phrases
in	**in** caves / **in** the water / **in** Australia
on	**on** a table / **on** the floor / **on** a leaf
at	**at** home / **at** school / **at** the park
between	**between** the tree and the river
near	**near** the zoo / **near** the plains
under	**under** the tree / **under** the desk
above	**above** the mountain / **above** the door

Practice

Complete the sentences with *on*, *at*, *between*, *under*, or *above*. Write the sentences.

Example: We have a rabbit <u>at</u> school.

1. We see squirrels _____ the park.

2. Birds are flying _____ the trees.

3. The camels walked _____ the sand.

4. The cat is hiding _____ the bed!

5. The zebras are _____ the trees and the river.

Apply

Work with a partner. Ask and answer the questions. Use prepositional phrases in your answers.

Example: A: What do you have on your desk?

        B: I have a notebook on my desk.

- What do you have on your desk?
- Where do you eat lunch?
- Where do you like to play with friends?
- What do you keep in your backpack?
- Where do you live?
- Where do you keep your toys and games?
- Where do you sit in class?
- Where do you do your homework?

86

Grammar Check ✓

Name a **preposition**. Use it in a sentence.

Writing

Write a Poem about an Animal

Ongoing
Writing
Skills
Practice

A poem can express ideas, information, and feelings. A good poem includes details that help the reader picture what is being described.

Writing Prompt

Write a poem about an animal. Tell facts about the animal.
Be sure to use prepositions and prepositional phrases correctly.

① Prewrite

Choose an animal to write about. Think about the animal's habits. What does the animal eat? Where does it live and sleep? List the facts in a Poem Chart.

A student named Antonio has started to list his ideas like this:

LINE 1:	I am a/an (animal).	I am a bat.
LINE 2:	I am as (color) as (noun).	I am as black as the night.
LINE 3:	I live in (place).	I live in caves and in tree tops.
LINE 4:	I eat (foods).	I eat insects and fruit.

② Draft

Use your Poem Chart to help you write a first draft.

- Keep in mind your purpose—to write a poem.
- Include interesting facts about your animal.

❸ Revise

Reread your draft. Look for places where it needs improvement. Use the Writing Checklist to help you find problems. Then revise your draft.

❹ Edit

Check your work for errors. Do Peer Review (use the Checklist on page 402).

❺ Publish

Make a clean copy of your final draft. Share it with the class. Save your work for the Writing Workshop.

Here is Antonio's poem:

Antonio Corrales

I am a bat.
I am as black as the night.
I live in caves and in tree tops.
I eat insects and fruit.
I sleep upside down during the day with other bats.
I can fly through the air.
I can see in the dark.
I am a bat.

87–88

Prepare to Read

What You Will Learn

Reading

■ Vocabulary building: *Context, word study*

■ Reading strategy: *Identify cause and effect*

■ Text type: *Informational text (photo essay)*

Grammar
Adjectives and adverbs

Writing
Write a friendly letter

These words will help you understand the reading.

Key Words

insect

habitats

camouflage

prey

patterns

moth

Key Words

Can You See Them? tells how animals use camouflage.

Words in Context

1 This is an insect. An insect has three body parts, six legs, and antennae. Insects may also have wings.

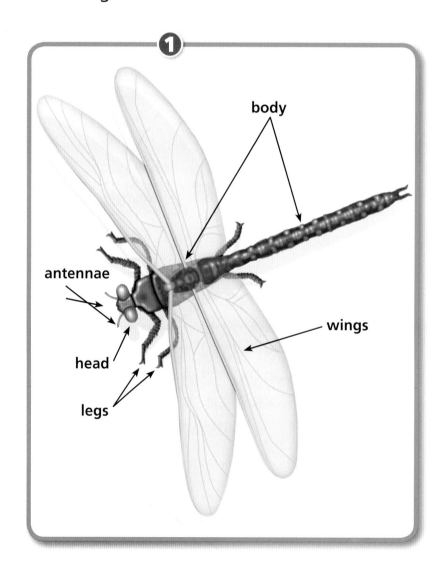

1

body

antennae

head

legs

wings

② Habitats are where animals live. Animals use camouflage to hide in their habitats. They hide from other animals that might eat them. Also, animals hide so they can catch prey. Prey is any animal that another animal eats.

③ The patterns on the pepper moth help it hide on a tree.

Practice

Make flashcards to help you memorize the words.

- Write a key word on the front.
- On the back, write the meaning.

Make Connections

Some animals use camouflage to be safe. People wear seat belts in cars to be safe. What do you do to be safe?

Speaking Skills

When you don't know the right word to use, explain or describe the idea using words you know.

89

These words will help you talk about the reading.

Academic Words

environment
world of land, sea, and air that something lives in

enable
make someone or something able to do something

Academic Words

Words in Context

Frogs need to live in a wet **environment**.

Wings **enable** birds to fly.

 **Practice**

Write the sentences in your notebook. Choose an academic word to complete each sentence.

1. People should keep the _____ clean.

2. Reading books will _____ you to learn about animals.

 **Apply**

Ask and answer with a partner.

1. What is a good **environment** for a pet?

2. What **enables** flowers to grow?

WB
90

Word Study

Compound Nouns

Compound nouns are made up of two smaller words.

frogmouth	sandhill	cottontail
frog + mouth	sand + hill	cotton + tail

Rule

Look for this pattern in English: sometimes two nouns join to form a new noun. These new nouns are called *compound nouns*.

Practice

Work with a partner. Take turns.

Reading Skill

Looking for patterns in English will make you a better reader.

- Read the sentences.
- List the compound nouns.
- Show the two words that make up each compound noun.

    1. Squirrels live in the woodlands.

    2. Owls sleep during the daylight.

    3. At nightfall, raccoons come out to look for food.

WB
91

INFORMATIONAL TEXT

Photo Essay

More About

THE BIG QUESTION

Why is it important to know how animals use camouflage?

Audio **Listen to the Audio.**
Listen for the general meaning. Think about the situation or context. Use this to help you understand the selection.

Reading Strategy

Identify Cause and Effect

Identifying cause and effect helps you understand how things are connected.

- As you read, look for causes—things that make other things happen.

- Look for effects—things that happen because of something else.

Listen as your teacher models the reading strategy.

Can You See Them?

by Kendra Clay

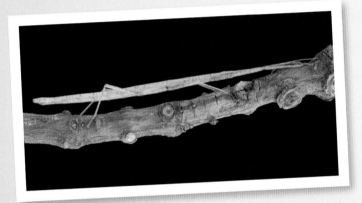

Can you see the insect in the photograph above? You will need to look carefully.

The insect is called a walking stick. It can hide in a tree because it looks like a small branch, or stick.

Arctic foxes live where the weather is very cold. They can change color. In summer, the foxes are brown. In winter, they are white.

A tawny frogmouth is a bird. It sits very still in a tree. It waits for prey to come near. Then it **pounces**!

Many animals hide. They may hide to keep safe from **predators**. Or, they may hide so they can catch prey.

This kind of hiding is called camouflage. When animals have camouflage, they are hard to see in their habitats.

---

pounces   jumps suddenly after waiting

predators   animals that kill and eat other animals

Patterns help this moth stay safe. Look at the big spots on the moth's wings. They look like a large animal's eyes. Predators stay away from this insect.

Before You Go On   Why does the tawny frogmouth stay very still?

A horned lizard is the color of the ground. The lizard can quickly change from a light color to a dark color. The insects it eats do not know it is there.

A Bengal tiger is a very large cat. It's hard for a big animal to hide. But the tiger has stripes. When it rests in the forest, its stripes blend in with the plants.

Sandhill cranes **migrate** south from Canada and Alaska. These gray-and-white birds blend in with the snowy lands around them.

---

migrate   move from one area to another as the seasons change

A leaf-tailed gecko is a kind of lizard. It blends in with a tree branch in Africa. It waits for prey to fly by.

This cottontail rabbit hides in some leaves on the ground in the forest. It must hide from predators.

92–94

Reading Strategy

Identify Cause and Effect

- Did you find out why some animals use camouflage?

- How did looking for cause and effect help you understand the selection?

Think It Over

1. **Recall** In what kind of climate do arctic foxes live?

2. **Comprehend** What does camouflage **enable** animals to do?

3. **Analyze** What role does **environment** play in an animal's ability to hide?

Learning Strategies

Cause and Effect

One thing can make another thing happen. The **cause** is the thing that happens first. The **effect** is the thing that happens because of the first thing.

Practice

Match each effect with its cause.

Cause	Effect
1. The Bengal tiger has stripes.	a. It can hide in a tree.
2. The Arctic fox lives where there is snow.	b. It can hide in the forest.
3. The walking stick insect looks like a small branch.	c. It can hide in the winter when its coat turns white.

Use a Cause and Effect Chart

Use a Cause and Effect Chart to show how  helps animals.

Practice

Copy this chart.

- Fill in the effects.
- Add two more causes. Fill in their effects.

Cause	Effect
The Bengal tiger has stripes.	It can hide in the forest.
The Arctic fox lives where there is snow.	
The walking stick looks like a branch.	

95

Apply

Summarize the selection to a partner.

Extension

Utilize Draw a picture of yourself as an animal. Label the picture to show how your camouflage helps you to stay safe. Share your drawing with the class.

Grammar

Adjectives and Adverbs

An **adjective** describes a noun. Adjectives give details about size, shape, color, and number.

the **rough** bark	a **busy** day
a **funny** joke	**three** horses
a **long** tail	**new** friends
delicious desserts	the **blue** sweater

In sentences, adjectives can go just **before** a noun or **after** a noun + a *be* verb.

Before a noun	After a noun + *be* verb
The moth has **big** <u>spots</u>. ⟶	Those <u>spots</u> **are** big.
Look at the **brown** <u>insect</u>. ⟶	The <u>insect</u> **is** brown.
Do you like **cold** <u>weather</u>? ⟶	The <u>weather</u> **is** cold.

An **adverb** modifies a **verb**, an **adjective**, or another **adverb**. Many adverbs answer the question *How?* These adverbs often end in *–ly*.

Adverbs ending in *-ly*:	Other adverbs:
You need to look **carefully**.	The weather is very **cold**.
The lizard can **quickly** change.	The tiger is quite **dangerous**.
The gecko waits **quietly** for a meal.	

Practice

Circle the adjectives or adverbs in the sentences. Write the sentences.

Example: The (green) gecko is hiding.

1. The tiger has black stripes.

2. The moth is still.

3. The brown rabbit hid in the leaves.

4. The lizard quickly changed color.

5. The bird pounced suddenly on its prey.

Apply

Work with a partner. Ask and answer the questions. Use adjectives and adverbs in your sentences.

Example: A: What color is your hair?

B: My hair is brown.

- What color is your hair?
- What kind of weather do you like?
- What does your friend's dog look like?
- Do you have a big collection of anything?
- Do you walk quickly or slowly?
- Do you talk loudly or softly?
- Do you exercise daily or weekly?
- Do you ride your bike carefully or carelessly?

96

Grammar Check ✓

Name one **adjective** and one **adverb**. Use each one in a sentence.

Writing

Write a Friendly Letter

When you write a letter, you must think about your audience. Who will be reading your letter? This will affect your choice of words and language structures.

Writing Prompt

Write a letter to a friend or family member. Use informal language. Talk about something that you are learning in school. Be sure to use adjectives and adverbs correctly.

❶ Prewrite

Choose an animal or insect to write about. Think about its physical characteristics and/or habits. Then think about what these characteristics allow it to do. List the facts in a chart.

A student named Iman listed his ideas like this:

> **Characteristic:** Looks like a stick.
> **What this means:** Uses camouflage to hide.

> **Characteristic:** Very light.
> **What this means:** Can walk on water.

> **Characteristic:** Has suction cups on feet.
> **What this means:** Can climb and walk upside down.

❷ Draft

Use your chart to help you write a first draft.

- Keep in mind your purpose–to write a friendly letter.
- Include interesting facts about your animal or insect.

❸ Revise

Reread your draft. Look for places where it needs improvement. Use the Writing Checklist to help you find problems. Then revise your draft.

❹ Edit

Check your work for errors. Do Peer Review (use the Checklist on page 402).

❺ Publish

Make a clean copy of your final draft. Share it with the class. Save your work for the Writing Workshop.

Here is Miguel's letter:

Writing Checklist

Ideas

✔ I included facts in my letter.
✔ I expressed my ideas clearly.

Conventions

✔ I used adjectives correctly.
✔ I used adverbs correctly.

41 Oak Road
Bigtown, MD 09050
March 14, 2011

Dear Grandma,

I learned about a really interesting insect in school today. Have you ever seen a walking stick? It's an insect that looks exactly like a tree branch or twig. It uses camouflage, so birds can't find it. A walking stick moves very slowly. Amazingly, it can walk on water! It has claws and suction cups on its feet, so it can walk upside down. Isn't that cool?

Love,
Miguel

97–98

Reading 3

Prepare to Read

What You Will Learn

Reading
- Vocabulary building: *Context, phonics*
- Reading strategy: *Identify sequence*
- Text type: *Informational text (science)*

Grammar
Adverbs of time

Writing
Write a personal narrative

These words will help you understand the reading.

Key Words

- **butterfly**
- **leaf**
- **hatch**
- **caterpillar**
- **cocoon**
- **tadpole**

Key Words

How Do They Grow? tells how a butterfly and a frog change as they grow.

Words in Context *Audio*

A butterfly changes as it grows.

1 It starts as an egg on a leaf.

2 The egg begins to hatch.

3 A caterpillar comes out of the egg. It eats and eats.

4 Then the caterpillar hangs from a leaf.

5 It builds a cocoon around itself.

6 A butterfly comes out of the cocoon.

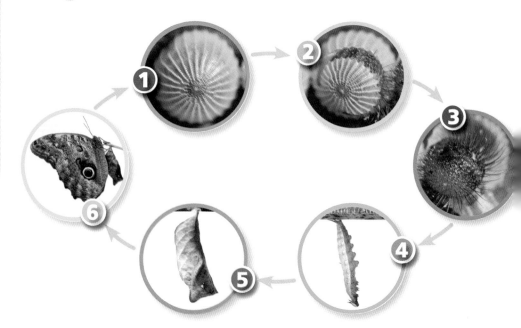

A frog also changes. A tadpole is
a baby frog. It changes into a frog
when it grows up.

(**Practice**)

**Draw pictures of the key words. Label each picture with a
sentence that contains the key word.**

Make Connections

Some animals change as they grow. How do you change
as you grow? How do you feel about these changes?
After you discuss these questions, write your responses
in your notebook.

99

These words will help you talk about the reading.

Academic Words

occurs
happens

transform
completely change

Academic Words

Words in Context

When the eggs break open, something special **occurs**. Baby chicks are born.

A small caterpillar **transforms** into a beautiful butterfly.

Practice

Write the sentences in your notebook. Choose an academic word to complete each sentence.

1. Water ____ into ice when you put it in the freezer.

2. What ____ when you mix red and white paint?

Apply

Ask and answer with a partner.

1. What are some things that **occur** at your school every day?

2. If you could **transform** yourself into an animal, which animal would you be? Explain.

WB
100

Phonics

Digraphs: *ch, sh, th*

Sometimes when two consonants are together, they make a new sound. Listen. Then read each word aloud.

ch	sh	th
change	ship	then
branch	wish	both

Rule

The letters *ch*, *sh*, and *th* come together to make one sound. This new sound is called a *digraph*.

Practice

Work with a partner. Take turns.

- Read the sentences.
- List the words with *ch, sh,* or *th*.
- Circle the letters *ch, sh,* or *th* in the words.

1. Living things may change.

2. Fish hatch from eggs.

3. Snakes shed their skin.

4. Silkworms become moths.

101

INFORMATIONAL TEXT

Science

More About

Why should people care how animals change as they grow?

Listen to the Audio.
Listen for the general meaning. Think about the situation or context. Use this to help you understand the selection.

Reading Strategy

Recognize Sequence

Recognizing the **sequence**, or order, of events helps you understand the text.

- As you read, pay attention to the order in which events happen.
- Look for words that show sequence, such as *first*, *next*, *then*, and *finally*.

Listen as your teacher models the reading strategy.

How Do They Grow?

by Leila Han

Learn about how some animals grow and change.

This frog was not always big and brown. This butterfly did not always have bright wings.

Living things grow and change. Sometimes the change is **dramatic,** and the living thing experiences a transformation.

Let's look at the transformations that occur in the lives of butterflies and frogs.

---

dramatic   very noticeable or surprising

Butterfly

First, a butterfly must find a place to lay eggs. A leaf is a good place.

Soon an egg will hatch, and a tiny caterpillar will crawl out. The caterpillar starts to eat right away. It **munches** on plants.

Next, the caterpillar builds a cocoon around itself. The cocoon sticks to a tree branch. It hangs there and does not move. But changes happen inside.

Then the butterfly breaks out of the cocoon. It spreads its wings and is ready to fly.

_____

munches   chews

Before You Go On   What **occurs** inside the cocoon?

Frog

A frog lays eggs in the water. Soon, an egg hatches. A tiny tadpole **wiggles** out.

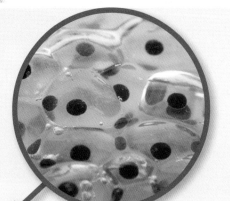

Reading Skill

If you don't understand something, ask your classmates or your teacher for help.

A tadpole lives in the water. It is very **vulnerable**. It must depend on its camouflage to **survive**.

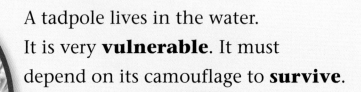

It starts to grow legs. The tadpole's legs grow and grow. Finally, when the tadpole is developed enough, it can leave the water.

---

wiggles   moves from side to side
vulnerable   has no protection
survive   to continue to live

Now the tadpole is a frog. The frog can hop on land. It can swim in the water, too.

WB 102–104

Reading Strategy

Identify Sequence

- What **sequence** words did you find in the selection?
- How does identifying the sequence help you understand the selection?

Think It Over

1. **Recall** Where does a tadpole live?
2. **Comprehend** How does a caterpillar **transform** into a butterfly? Explain.
3. **Analyze** How are the butterfly and the frog similar?

Learning Strategies

Steps in a Process

A **process** is something that happens in order. The parts of a process are called **steps**.

Practice

The list below shows steps that occur **during a frog's** transformation. **Put the steps in the right order.**

- The frog hops on land.
- The frog lays eggs in the water.
- The tadpole wiggles out.
- The egg hatches.
- The tadpole grows legs.

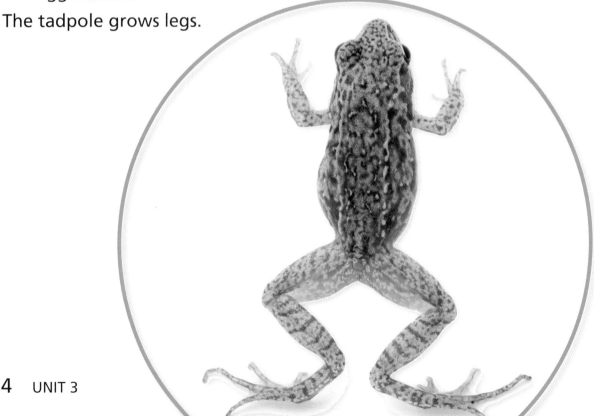

Use a Sequence Chart

A Sequence Chart can help you put steps in a process in the right order.

 G.O. 144

This Sequence Chart shows some steps in the life of a butterfly.

1. Which step should be in Box 3?
    a. A butterfly comes out of the egg.
    b. A tadpole comes out of the egg.
    c. A caterpillar comes out of the egg.
    d. A cocoon comes out of the egg.

2. If there were a Box 6, which step would it be?
    a. The butterfly becomes a caterpillar.
    b. The butterfly spreads its wings.
    c. The butterfly makes a cocoon.
    d. The butterfly becomes a tadpole.

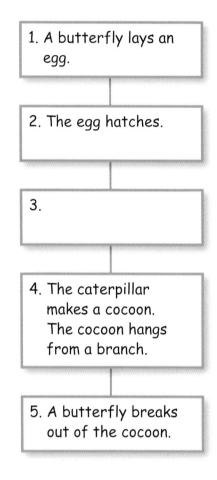

1. A butterfly lays an egg.

2. The egg hatches.

3.

4. The caterpillar makes a cocoon. The cocoon hangs from a branch.

5. A butterfly breaks out of the cocoon.

105

Apply

Retell the selection to a partner.

Extension

Utilize Think of something you do in steps. It can be tying your shoes or brushing your teeth. Make a Sequence Chart. Show the steps you do. Share the chart with your class and explain the steps.

Grammar

Adverbs of Time

An **adverb of time** is a word that describes when something happens. Things can occur in the past, present, or future.

> Yesterday, I saw a butterfly.

Adverbs of Time	Examples
now	**Now** the tadpole is a frog.
before	I get home **before** my brother does.
soon	**Soon** it will be spring.
early	I left school **early**.
today	**Today** I have gym.
tomorrow	**Tomorrow** I will finish my project.
later	I will meet you there **later**.
again	Let's come here **again**.

Review these common **adverbs of time** and how they are used in sentences.

Adverbs of time can also show the order, or sequence, of things that happen. They connect one sentence to the next.

Step 1	⟶	First, a butterfly lays eggs.
Step 2	⟶	Next, the eggs hatch and a caterpillar crawls out.
Step 3	⟶	Then, the caterpillar builds a cocoon.
Step 4	⟶	Finally, a butterfly breaks out.

Practice

Circle the adverb of time in each sentence.

Write the sentences.

Example: (Yesterday) I visited my grandparents.

1. I will look for caterpillars today.

2. I'll be finished with the computer soon.

3. I do sit-ups before I go to sleep.

4. Let's review these questions later.

5. How early do I have to get up?

Apply

Work with a partner. Ask and answer the questions.
Use adverbs of time in your responses.

Example: A: When do you have lunch?
B: I have lunch after math.

- When do you have lunch?

- When do you have English?

- How early do you go to sleep on week nights?

- How soon will you graduate from high school?

- Are you hungry now?

- Will you go to the library later?

- What did you do yesterday?

- What will you do tomorrow?

106

Grammar Check ✓

Name an **adverb of time.** Use it in a sentence.

Writing

Write a Personal Narrative

In a personal narrative, you tell about an event or an experience that was important to you.

Writing Prompt

Write a paragraph about an important event in your life. Give details about your experience and explain how you felt. Be sure to use adverbs of time correctly.

❶ Prewrite G.O. 141

Choose an event to write about. Tell about what happened and how you felt. List your ideas in a Details Chart.

A student named Maki listed her ideas like this:

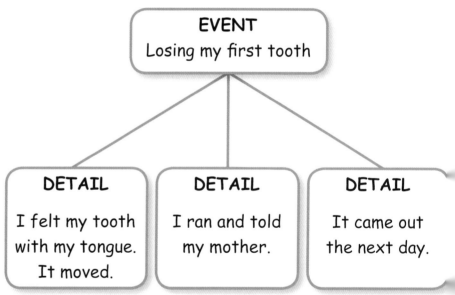

❷ Draft

Use your Details Chart to help you write a first draft.

- Keep in mind your purpose—to write a paragraph about a memorable event.

- Include details about what happened and how you felt.

❸ Revise

Reread your draft. Look for places where it needs improvement. Use the Writing Checklist to help you find problems. Then revise your draft.

❹ Edit

Check your work for errors. Do Peer Review (use the Checklist on page 402).

❺ Publish

Make a clean copy of your final draft. Share it with the class. Save your work for the Writing Workshop.

Here is Maki's story:

Maki Umemoto

The Day I Lost My First Tooth

I remember when I lost my first baby tooth. I was five years old. One day, I felt my tooth with my tongue. It was loose! I was so excited. I ran and showed my mother. The next day, I was eating a sandwich. I put my tongue where my loose tooth was, but it was gone! My mother and I looked everywhere for it. Finally, I found it. It was in my sandwich!

Writing Checklist

Ideas

✔ I included important details about what happened.

✔ I expressed my ideas clearly.

Conventions

✔ I used adverbs of time correctly.

✔ I used the past tense correctly.

107–108

Apply and Extend

Link the Readings

Copy the chart into your notebook. Read the words in the top row.

- For *Animals at Home/Little Allie Alligator*, put an X under the words that remind you of the poems.

- Repeat the same activity for the other readings.

	Informational text	Literature	Survival	Habitat / environment
Animals at Home / Little Allie Alligator				
Can You See Them?				
How do they grow?				

Discussion

1. What animals do the two poems talk about?

2. How do some animals camouflage themselves in their **environment**? Why do they do it?

3. What changes **occur** when butterflies and frogs begin to **transform**?

 What can we learn about animals and why is learning about them important?

> **Listening Skills**
>
> If you can't hear someone, you can say, "Could you speak more loudly, please?"

Projects

Your teacher will help you choose one of these projects.

Written	Oral	Visual/Active
Animal Facts	**Guessing Game**	**Diorama**
Choose an animal that you like. Write three facts about it. Tell where it lives, what it eats, and what it looks like.	Make a list of facts about an animal. Tell what it eats and where it lives. Have a partner guess the animal.	Make a diorama. Show sky, land, and water. Show animals where they live. Share your diorama with the class.
Animal Story	**Talk About It**	**Habitat Mobile**
Write a story about an animal. Tell about its home. Tell how the animal found its home.	Find out about an animal that uses camouflage to stay safe. Give a formal presentation about the animal to your class.	Make a mobile. Show pictures of animals in their homes. Write a fact on the back of each picture.

Further Reading

For more projects visit
LongmanCornerstone.com.

Animals

Meet some exciting wild animals and their babies in this Penguin Young Reader. What are they like and what do they eat?

Animal Dads, Sneed B. Collard III

Books about parenting in the animal world often focus on the mothers' role. But here, it's all about fathers. Beautiful, cut paper collages show these animals in their natural habitats.

109–110

Listening and Speaking Workshop

Recite a Poem

You are going to write and recite a poem. Then you will listen as your classmates recite their poems.

❶ Prepare

A. Choose a favorite activity or animal. You will write a poem about it and recite it to the class. Your classmates will tell you how your poem makes them feel.

B. Recall what you know about your favorite activity or animal. Then write your poem about it.

> One day,
> Eating a leaf, all green and new.
> One day,
> Looking at the sky, all big and blue.
> One day,
> Going to fly, all pretty like you!

❷ Practice

Practice your poem until you have memorized it. Practice in front of your family or friends. If possible, record your presentation. Then listen to yourself. How do you sound? Record yourself again and try to improve.

❸ Present

As you speak, do the following:

- Speak clearly and with feeling.
- If you forget a word, don't worry! Just go on with your poem.
- After your poem, ask your classmates how it made them feel.

As you listen, do the following:

- Listen to how your classmate speaks with feeling and expression.
- Listen carefully for ideas and information that is implied, or not stated directly.
- Write down any new words you hear.

❹ Evaluate

After you speak, answer these questions:

- ✓ Did you memorize your poem?
- ✓ Did you speak with feeling?

After you listen, answer these questions:

- ✓ What was the poem about?
- ✓ How did the poem make you feel?
- ✓ Think about the general meaning of the poem. Can you think of a title for it? Tell your idea to the class.

Writing Workshop

Write a Personal Narrative

Writing Prompt
Write a personal narrative. Give details about something you experienced. Say why the experience was important to you and what you learned from it. Speak directly to the reader. Be sure your narrative has a beginning, a middle, and an end.

❶ Prewrite
Review the writing you have done in this unit. Then choose something that happened to you to write about. List the details in a chart.

A student named May listed her ideas like this:

Event	Going to music camp
When	Last summer
Where	In Maine
Details	1. My mom said I should go to music camp in Maine. 2. My last experience at a camp was not good. 3. I loved the music camp.
How It Ended	I learned to give things a chance.

❷ Draft
Use your chart to help you write a first draft.

- Keep in mind your purpose—to write a personal narrative.
- Include why it was important or what you learned from it.

❸ Revise

Read your draft. Look for places where the writing needs improvement. Use the Writing Checklist to help you find problems. Then revise your draft.

Here is how May revised her essay:

Six Traits of Writing Checklist

✔ **Ideas**
Did I say why the experience was important to me?

✔ **Organization**
Does my narrative have a beginning, middle, and end?

✔ **Voice**
Do I speak directly to the reader?

✔ **Words**
Did I use words that will keep my readers interested?

✔ **Sentence Fluency**
Did I use different kinds of sentences?

✔ **Conventions**
Do I use negative forms correctly?

May Yang

Music Camp

Last
~~This~~ summer my mom sent me to music camp. I really didn't want to go. Why?

Two summers ago I went to a summer camp. I hated
it. The counselors ~~are~~ were strict and the kids weren't nice. I didn't have fun.

But this camp was different. The kids were very nice. The counselors weren't too strict. I was playing my guitar all day and doing other fun activities. I really enjoyed the rest of my time ~~in~~ at the camp.

I learned from this experience that I shouldn't decide about things before I do them. I have to give things a chance.

Revised to correct adverb of time.

Revised to correct verb tense.

Revised to add adverb for emphasis.

Revised to correct use of preposition.

④ Edit

Check your work for errors. Trade papers with a partner to get feedback. Use the Peer Review Checklist.

⑤ Publish

Make a clean copy of your final draft. Share it with the class.

111–112

Peer Review Checklist

✓ Events are told in a logical order.

✓ All the information is related to the topic.

✓ The narrative includes interesting details.

SPELLING TIP

A contraction is a word made from a verb and another word. Form a negative contraction with a verb + n't (an apostrophe replaces the o in *not*). For example *were* + *not* = *weren't*.

Listen to the sentences. Pay attention to **the groups of words. Read aloud.**

1. Animals share the world with us, as pets or wild and free.

2. Some animals use camouflage to be safe from predators.

3. Living things such as frogs and butterflies change as they grow.

Work in pairs. Take turns reading aloud the passage below for one minute. Count the number of words you read.

How Do They Grow? tells how a butterfly and a frog	11
grow and change over their lifetimes. The butterfly starts	20
as an egg, which then hatches to become a caterpillar. The	31
caterpillar surrounds itself in a cocoon and later changes	40
into a butterfly.	43
The frog also starts life as an egg, which then hatches to	55
become a little tadpole. Over time, the tadpole grows legs	66
and then moves from the water onto land. It is now a frog.	81
It can hop on land and swim in the water, too.	89

With your partner, find the words that slowed you down.

• Practice saying each word and then say the sentence each word is in.

• Then take turns reading the text again. Count the number of words you read.

113

Test Preparation

Taking Tests

You will often take tests that help show what you know. Follow these tips to improve your test-taking skills.

Coaching Corner

Answering Test Questions That Are Cloze Items

- A cloze passage is a reading selection that has blanks for you to fill in. Each blank will have a number. Then you will be given answer choices for each number. You need to choose which of the choices is best to complete the numbered blank in the passage.

- Remember to pay attention to the words and sentences before and after each blank in the passage. You will often find clues in the selection that will help you choose the best word to fill in the blank.

- After you read all the answer choices, think of each word in the blank and read the sentence aloud each time. Reading the sentence aloud will help you choose the word that makes the most sense.

Read the following test sample. Study the tips in the box.

115–116

Read the selection. Then choose the correct words to fill in the blanks.

The Traveling Tank

1   An armadillo is a small ___1___ whose back, head, legs, and tail are covered with bony plates of "armor." The name "armadillo" is a Spanish word that means "little armored one." These bands of armor give protection to the armadillo. If an armadillo feels unsafe, it will curl up into a ball until the danger is gone.

2   Armadillos have small eyes. They cannot see very well. Instead, they rely on their ___2___ sense of smell to hunt. An armadillo uses its sharp ___3___ and strong legs to dig for food. It uses its pointy snout and long, sticky tongue to find and eat all sorts of insects.

1 **A** flower
     B mammal
     C fish
     D tree

2 **F** weak
     G colorful
     H small
     J strong

3 **A** feet
     B face
     C claws
     D armor

Tips

✔ Read the whole selection before you try to fill in the blanks. This will give you a better idea of what information is missing.

✔ Use the information in the passage to create a picture of an armadillo in your head. Use this picture to help you answer the questions.

Great Ideas

Create art. Explore in science. Start with an idea and build on it. That's how we get great ideas.

Reading

1 Article

On Your Bike, Get Set, Donate!

2 Science

Scientists and Crows

3 Photo Essay

A Story to Tell

What are some great ideas that make our world a better place?

Listening and Speaking

You will talk about great ideas and inventions. In the Listening and Speaking Workshop, you will give a presentation.

Writing

You will practice expository writing. In the Writing Workshop, you will write to compare and contrast.

Quick Write

People can have great ideas in science and art. Make a list of other areas people can have great ideas in.

DVD

VIEW AND RESPOND

Talk about the poster for this unit. Then watch and listen to the video and answer the questions at LongmanCornerstone.com.

What do you know about people with great ideas?

Words to Know

Listen and repeat. Use these words to talk about people with great ideas.

 inventor

 actor

 writer

 builder

 painter

 gardener

Work with a partner. Look up these words in a dictionary. Then ask and answer questions.

act in plays	build houses	grow plants
paint pictures	write books	invent things

Example: A: What do <u>actors</u> do?

B: They <u>act in plays</u>.

Read the question. Write your response in your notebook.

Choose one of the jobs above. Write two or three sentences about it.

Make Connections

Copy the sentences into your notebook and complete them.

plays

painting

stories

gardens

inventions

buildings

1. Builders create these. They come in many different sizes. _____

2. The students at my school love to act. We create these every fall and spring. _____

3. My mom creates these in our backyard with flowers and vegetables. _____

4. I create these in art class. I use paints and brushes. _____

5. Writers create these so we can read or hear them. _____

6. Scientists create these. Sometimes it takes years and years to finish them. _____

What about you?

Talk with a partner. What do you like to create? What can your parents and brothers or sisters create?

Kids' Stories from around the World Audio

Vermont, U.S.A.

Allison

Most plants grow in dirt. In my school in Vermont, we are learning how to grow plants in water. We put food for the plants in the water. Scientists have grown plants this way. This can help countries that don't have much land. Farmers can use water to help them grow more food.

Colin

I am a reporter in England even though I am nine years old! I am part of a news group that is run by young people. We decide what to write about. Then we talk with people. Our stories are in newspapers, on websites, and on the radio.

Zarifa

I live in Azerbaijan. We have a museum of tiny books. There are more than 4,000 books. The biggest book is only 4 inches tall! A woman who loves books opened this museum.

England

France

Azerbaijan

Anton

Many people in my country, France, love to ski. Some schools in France teach people who are physically challenged how to ski. These people can take part in special races, too. This way, everyone can have fun in the snow!

What about you?

1. What is your great idea? (Remember, sometimes a great idea can be small.)

2. Do you have a story about someone else's great idea? Share your story.

What You Will Learn

Reading

- Vocabulary building: *Context, word study*

- Reading strategy: *Identify problems and solutions*

- Text type: Informational text *(magazine article)*

Grammar

need/want/like/love + to + verb

Writing

Describe a problem and solution

These words will help you understand the reading.

Key Words

donate

volunteers

bicycles

helmets

Key Words

On Your Bike, Get Set, Donate! is about groups that fix old bicycles to give to people who need them.

Words in Context

Audio

1 Each year, our school has a bake sale to raise money. We make cookies and cupcakes. Then we **donate** them to be sold. My friends and I are **volunteers** at the bake sale.

2 Bicycles are also called bikes. A bicycle has two wheels.

3 This girl and boy are wearing safety helmets.

Make flashcards to help you memorize the words.

- Write a key word on the front.
- On the back, write the meaning.

Make Connections

How can you ride a bicycle safely? What should you wear? Where should you ride? Use some of the key words as you speak.

WB
117

These words will help you talk about the reading.

Academic Words

Words in Context

Our bodies **benefit** from eating healthy food. It gives us more energy.

Normally the children walked to school, but today they can ride their new bikes.

Practice

Write the sentences in your notebook. Choose an academic word to complete each sentence.

1. We ____ from getting 8 or 9 hours of sleep every night. It helps our memory.

2. The post office is ____ open on Mondays, but today it is closed. It is a holiday.

Apply

Ask and answer with a partner.

1. Sometimes we make mistakes, like forgetting to bring our homework to school. How can we **benefit** from our mistakes? Give an example.

2. What do you **normally** do on Saturdays? What about last Saturday? Was it a typical Saturday?

WB
118

Word Study

Pronunciation of Ending -*ed* Audio

Listen. Then read aloud.

> The children **started** school.
> The boys **repaired** the bike.

The words *started* and *repaired* both tell about the past. But the ending -*ed* is pronounced differently in each word.

> start + ed = start/ed   repair + ed = repaired

Rule

Look for this pattern in English: if the letter *d* or the letter *t* comes before the -*ed* ending, then -*ed* is pronounced as a separate syllable.

Practice

Work with a partner. Take turns.

- Sound out the words in the box.

- Add -*ed* to each word. Read the new word aloud.

- Tell if the -*ed* adds a syllable to the word.

1. add
2. help
3. seat
4. play
5. show

WB
119

INFORMATIONAL TEXT

Magazine Article

More About

How can people use a great idea to help others?

 Listen to the Audio.
Listen for the main points and important details.

Reading Strategy

Identify Problems and Solutions

Identifying problems and solutions helps you understand a text better. To identify problems and solutions, follow these steps:

- What problems are described?
- What are the solutions, and who helps find them?

Listen as your teacher models the reading strategy.

On Your Bike, Get Set, DONATE!

by Jamaila Veglia

People like to ride bicycles. Every year, many Americans buy new bicycles. What happens to the old **bikes**? People throw away many of them. What a waste!

---

bikes   bicycles

These boys
can fix bikes.

A Great Idea

Bicycle riders can donate their old bikes to
groups of people who have a great idea. These
groups **fix** the bikes. Then the groups give the
bikes to children who don't
have bicycles. The groups may
give bikes to grown-ups who
need them, too. Some groups
send bicycles to people in
other countries.

_____

fix   make like new

Some groups
donate bicycles
to people in
other countries.

Before You Go On | In America, what **normally** happens to old bikes?

New riders learn bicycle safety.

Volunteers Help

Bicycle Exchange is a group that gives away bikes. Each year, people donate their old bikes to this group. People in Bicycle Exchange teach volunteers how to fix bikes. Then, the volunteers work to **repair** old bikes. At the end of the year, Bicycle Exchange gives bikes to children. The group also gives helmets to children. People in the group teach children bicycle safety, too. Children need to know how to ride and be safe.

A volunteer works to repair a bike.

---

repair fix

It can be fun to fix old bikes.

It can be fun to teach others how to fix bikes, too.

A Boy Helps Others

Young people can help, too. Joshua started fixing bikes when he was twelve years old. He gave them to children who did not have bicycles.

Joshua got started when his own bike broke. He had an idea. He would learn how to fix it himself. Soon, neighbors were bringing old bikes to Joshua's house. He repaired them. Now other children have new bikes.

Before You Go On What was Joshua's idea? How did others **benefit** from his idea?

A man rides a bicycle to work in Ghana.

Around the World

Groups send bicycles to countries where it is not easy to buy a bike. One group, Bikes for the World, sent 430 bikes to Togo. Many children must walk ten miles or more to get to school in Togo. Bikes can really help!

Another group, Bike Works, sends bikes to **villages** in Ghana. Farmers, teachers, and students use the bikes to get to work and to school.

---

villages   very small towns in the country

Riders Write Back

Volunteers love to hear from new bike riders. They like to know that their work makes people happy.

A group called Second Chance got a poem from one rider.

Bike Works got a note from a young girl in Ghana. "I love my bike," she wrote. "It is blue which is my **favorite** color."

---

favorite   one you like best

Bikes are tight.

They make me

Feel all right.

I love my bike.
It is blue which is
my favorite color.
Lakiska

WB
120–122

Reading Strategy

Identify Problems and Solutions

- What problem do people with old bikes have?
- What problem do people without bikes have?
- What solutions do people have for these problems?
- How did looking for problems and solutions help you understand the selection?

Think It Over

1. **Recall**   How does Bicycle Exchange help people?
2. **Comprehend**   What do Joshua and the other groups in this selection have in common?
3. **Analyze**   Why is it a waste to throw away an old bicycle?

Bicycles

▲ High-Wheel Bicycle

The high-wheel bicycle was first made in 1871. Riders cannot put their feet on the ground. How do you think that would feel?

Unicycle ▶

It takes a lot of practice to ride this unicycle! Do you think you could ride it?

▲ Tricycle

A tricycle has three wheels. Small children can ride tricycles.

Delivery Bike ▲

The basket on this bike can hold things. A rider could use this bike to take packages to people.

▲ BMX Bikes

These girls race on BMX bikes. Riders can do tricks and ride on dirt roads with these bikes.

Mountain Bike ▶

This man is riding a mountain bike. These bikes go on dirt trails or bumpy roads. They have wide tires.

▲ Wheelchair Cycle

This man can ride or race on this wheelchair cycle.

Activity to Do

These two pages use words and pictures to tell about bicycles.

- Choose another machine used for travel.
- Find pictures to show that machine.
- Post your pictures with captions in your classroom.

Learning Strategies

Problems and Solutions

A magazine article can tell how people find solutions to problems.

Practice

Read these sentences about the selection. Tell which sentences are problems. Tell which sentences are solutions.

1. Many people throw away old bikes.
2. Many children do not have bicycles.
3. Bicycle Exchange volunteers teach people how to fix old bikes.
4. Groups give repaired bicycles to people who need them.
5. In many countries, it is not easy to buy a bike.

Use a T-Chart

You can use a T-Chart to help you understand the selection.

G.O.
149

Copy the chart. Use the steps below to see how each group or person solved the problems in the selection.

Group or Person	Solution
Bicycle Exchange	_____ _____
Joshua	_____ _____
_____	_____ _____

- List two or more things Bicycle Exchange does to solve the problems.
- List two or more things Joshua does to solve the problems.
- List one more group. Tell one thing the group does to solve the problems.

Summarize the selection for a partner.
Use some of the key words.

123

Extension

Utilize Choose one thing that you could give away. Draw a picture of it. Write about why someone else might want it. Present your idea to the class.

Grammar

Need/Want/Like/Love + to + Verb

The verbs *need*, *want*, *like*, and *love* are often followed by *to* + **verb**.

> Volunteers love to hear from new bike riders.

Read the sentences in this chart.

Subject	Verb + *to* + Verb
Volunteers	love to hear from new bike riders.
She	likes to know that she helped.
Children	need to learn about their bicycles.
Joshua	wants to fix bikes for others.
I	want to help.

To make **negative sentences**, add *do not*, *does not*, *did not*, or *will not* before *need, want, like,* or *love*. You can use contractions.

Affirmative	Negative
She **needs to buy** it. ⟶	She **does not need to buy** it.
	She **doesn't need to buy** it.
I want **to donate** it. ⟶	I **do not want to donate** it.
	I **don't want to donate** it.

Complete the sentences with *to* + verb.

Write the sentences. Use words from the box.

> donate   answer   wear   close   finish   ride

Example: Some kids love <u>to ride</u> bicycles.

1. He doesn't like _____ the questions.

2. They need _____ helmets when they ride.

3. We don't want _____ the window.

4. I need _____ my homework.

5. They want _____ their bikes to people in need.

Apply

Work with a partner. Ask and answer the questions.

Use *to* + verb in your answers.

Example: A: What do you want to do after school?

B: I want to play baseball after school.

124

- What do you want to do after school?
- Do you like to listen to music?
- Do you need to finish your homework?
- Where do you like to go on the weekend?
- What shows do you love to watch on TV?
- What games to you like to play?

**Grammar
Check ✓**

Use *like* + *to* + **verb** in a sentence.

Writing

Describe a Problem and Solution

Ongoing Writing Skills Practice

Expository writing is writing that gives information or explains something. One example of expository writing is a problem and solution paragraph.

Writing Prompt

Write about a problem you or someone you know had and how it was solved. Be sure to use verb + *to* + infinitive correctly.

❶ Prewrite G.O. 149

Choose a situation to write about. Tell about what the problem was and how it was solved. List your ideas in a T-chart.

A student named Kabir listed his ideas like this:

PROBLEM	SOLUTION
I lost my backpack.	My friend helped me. He asked me to think when I last had it. I thought about it, and then I remembered. I had it in my karate class.

❷ Draft

Use your T-chart to help you write a first draft.

- Keep in mind your purpose—to describe a problem and how it was solved.
- Include details about what the problem was and how it was solved.

❸ Revise

Reread your draft. Look for places where it needs improvement. Use the Writing Checklist to help you find problems. Then revise your draft.

❹ Edit

Check your work for errors. Use the Peer Review Checklist on page 402.

❺ Publish

Make a clean copy of your final draft. Share it with the class. Save your work for the Writing Workshop.

Here is Kabir's story about his problem:

Writing Checklist

Ideas

✔ I described the problem and the solution.

✔ I expressed my ideas clearly.

Conventions

✔ I used verb + *to* + verb correctly.

✔ I used the past tense correctly.

✔ Subjects and verbs agree.

WB
125–126

Kabir Matwani

Last week, I lost my red backpack. I looked at home and at school. I needed to find it before the weekend. I had to study for two big tests. My friend Aidan wanted to help me. He asked me, "When did you last have it? What did you do? Where did you go?" I thought and thought. Then I remembered. I had it when I went to my karate class. Maybe I left it there! I went to the karate classroom. There was my red backpack. I was so happy!

Prepare to Read

What You Will Learn

Reading

- Vocabulary building: *Context, phonics*

- Reading strategy: *Identify main ideas and details*

- Text type: *Informational text (science)*

Grammar
Simple past: irregular verbs

Writing
Respond to text

These words will help you understand the reading.

Key Words

- instinct
- proof
- tool
- scientists
- lab

Key Words

In *Scientists and Crows,* you will read about how scientists study crows.

Words in Context

1 Babies cry when they are hungry or tired. They cry to show they need help. No one teaches babies how to cry. They know by instinct.

2 How do I know the kitten took the toy bird? This photo is the proof.

3 A rake is a tool that people use in a garden.

4 Jane Goodall is a scientist. She studies chimpanzees in their habitat.

5 George Washington Carver was a famous scientist. In this picture, he is working in a lab.

Make flashcards to help you memorize the words.

- Write a key word on the front.
- On the back, write a sentence, but leave a blank where the key word should be.

Make Connections

Think of a pet that you know. It could belong to you or someone else. How smart do you think the pet is? Why do you think so?

These words will help you talk about the reading.

Academic Words

method
a way of doing something

theory
unproven idea that explains something

Academic Words

Words in Context Audio

My **method** for learning new words is to write them in my vocabulary notebook.

Can plants grow without sunlight? Our **theory** is they can't. We'll do an experiment to find out.

Practice

Write the sentences in your notebook. Choose an academic word to complete each sentence.

1. The scientist has a _____ that explains why more people get sick in the winter.

2. Our dad uses a special _____ to wake us up in the morning. He turns the light in our room on and off several times.

Apply

Ask and answer with a partner.

1. How do you study for exams? Do you study alone or with friends? Talk about what **method** works best for you.

2. Why do people smile when they are happy? Think of a **theory** that could explain this.

Phonics

R-Controlled Vowels: *ir, er, ur*

The letter *r* after a vowel gives the vowel a new sound. Listen. Then read each word aloud.

bid	gem	hut
bird	germ	hurt

Rule

The letters *ir*, *er*, and *ur* usually have the same vowel sound.

Practice

Work with a partner.

- Sort the words in the box into three lists:
  - words with *ir*
  - words with *er*
  - words with *ur*

dirt	curb	herd
fern	her	perch
first	hurt	third
fur	girl	turn

- Sound out the words in your lists.
- Add a new word to each list.

INFORMATIONAL TEXT

Science

More About

THE BIG QUESTION

How can people try out their ideas to learn new things?

Audio Listen to the Audio.
Listen for the main points and important details.

Reading Strategy

Identify Main Idea and Details

The main idea is the most important idea in a selection. Details are the facts or pieces of information that support or explain the main idea.

- As you read, look for the main idea of the selection.
- Look for details that tell about the main idea.

Listen as your teacher models the reading strategy.

Scientists and Crows

**by Remore Williams
illustrated by Laura Jacobsen**

Do you ever watch crows? You may see crows fly over trees. You may see a crow sit on a power line. Maybe you hear crows call, "Caw! Caw! Caw!"

Scientists watch crows, too. They watch what crows do in their habitat. They also study crows in labs. Scientists study crows to learn more about them.

Crows and Clams

Crows eat clams. Clams are small animals that live inside a **shell**. The shell is hard. How can a crow eat an animal inside a shell? Some scientists in Japan studied some crows to find out.

The scientists watched crows eating clams. The crows picked up the clams with their beaks. They carried the clams high in the air, and then dropped them to the ground. When the shells hit the ground, they broke. Then the crows ate the clams.

---

shell   hard outer part

Before You Go On   What **method** did the crows use to open clams?

Crows and Walnuts

Crows eat walnuts, too. Walnuts are **nuts** that have very hard shells. How can a crow break the shell? The scientists learned by watching this, too.

Some crows dropped walnuts on a street. Cars drove over the shells and **cracked** them. Then the crows ate the nuts.

Sometimes a crow did not drop the walnuts. Sometimes a crow carried a walnut, put it down in a **crosswalk**, and flew away. Cars drove over the walnut and cracked the shell. Then the crow came back and ate the walnut.

---

nuts   dry fruit inside shells

cracked   broke the outside part to get what was inside

crosswalk   a marked place to cross a street

Reading Skill

As you read, use the pictures to help you understand words or ideas. Discuss these words or ideas with your partner.

Scientists know that birds do many things by instinct. For example, they learn to fly by instinct. But the crows in Japan seemed to be solving a problem. How could the scientists find out if the crows were using instinct or solving a problem?

The scientists had a great idea. They would test crows in a lab. They would try to learn if a crow could solve a problem. They would find the proof.

Before You Go On What **methods** did the crows use to open walnuts?

A crow lifts a bucket
with a bent wire.

Crows in a Lab

The scientists gave the crows this problem. They put
food in a tiny bucket with a handle. The bucket was at the
bottom of a tube. The crows could not reach the bucket
without using a tool.

Scientists gave the crows two wires. One wire was
straight. The other wire was bent, like a hook. A crow
could lift the bucket with the bent wire.

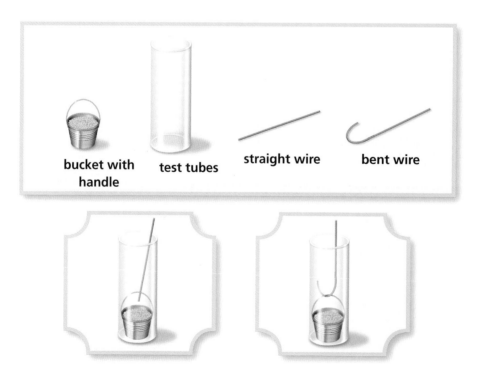

bucket with
handle

test tubes

straight wire

bent wire

A crow named Betty used the bent wire to lift the bucket four times.

Then, the scientists took away the bent wire. Betty tried to use the straight wire to lift the bucket. It didn't work. Betty needed a hook.

This crow pokes a stick into a rotting log to find insects to eat.

Then, Betty bent the wire herself. She lifted the bucket out of the tube with her new tool. Betty had made the right tool for the job!

Scientists learned that Betty the crow could solve a problem. This is not proof that all crows can solve problems. Scientists have to do more tests. They have to study other crows. But scientists used a great idea to learn something new about crows.

WB
130–132

Reading Strategy

Identify Main Ideas and Details

- What is the main idea?
- What details tell about the main idea?
- How did looking for the main idea help you understand the selection?

Think It Over

1. **Recall** What did Betty the crow do in the lab?

2. **Comprehend** What **theory** were scientists testing in the lab?

3. **Analyze** Some crows dropped walnuts in the street. Betty bent a wire. What do these two actions have in common?

Learning Strategies

Main Idea and Details

The **main idea** is the most important idea in a selection.
Details give important information to support the main
idea. **Support** means to help show something is true.

Practice

Read these sentences about the selection.

- Tell which one is the main idea.
- Tell which ones are details that support the main idea.

1. Crows crack walnuts by putting them in the street.

2. Crows break clams by dropping them on the ground.

3. Scientists study crows in their habitat and in labs.

4. In a lab, a crow bent a wire to get food.

Use a Main Idea and Details Chart

This chart can help you figure out the main idea of the selection. You can show the details that support the main idea.

 G.O.
141

Copy the chart. Fill in the main idea and details.

- What is the main idea of *Scientists and Crows*?
- Reread the selection. Find three details that support the main idea.

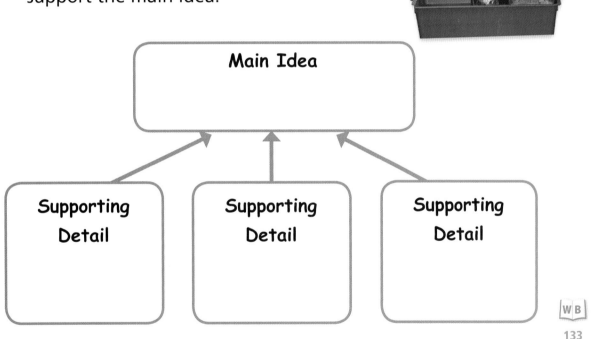

Main Idea

Supporting Detail

Supporting Detail

Supporting Detail

WB
133

Reread the selection and take notes. Then close your book and summarize the selection for a partner.

Extension

Utilize What animal would you like to study? What would you like to learn about the animal? Talk with a partner about how you would find out more about that animal.

Grammar

Simple Past: Irregular Verbs

Some verbs have an irregular past tense form.

> The crows **eat** the nuts. ⟶ The crows **ate** the nuts.

Review these **common irregular verbs** from the reading.

break ⟶ broke	find ⟶ found	know ⟶ knew
come ⟶ came	fly ⟶ flew	see ⟶ saw
drive ⟶ drove	give ⟶ gave	sit ⟶ sat

Make the past **negative** form of irregular verbs with *did not* (or *didn't*) and the plain form of the verb. Make **Yes-No and Wh- questions** with *did* and the plain form of the verb.

Affirmative	The car **drove** over the walnuts.
Negative	The car **didn't drive** over the walnuts.
Yes-No Question	**Did** scientists **find** the truth?
Wh- Question	Who **did** they **ask**?

Practice

Change each irregular verb to the past tense. Write the sentences.

Example: The crows sit on the power line.

The crows sat on the power line.

1. The clams break on the ground.

2. The crow flies away.

3. Do scientists know much about crows?

4. A scientist takes the tool from Betty.

5. Scientists see Betty solve the problem.

Apply

Work with a partner. Ask and answer the questions. Use irregular simple past verbs in your answers.

Example: A: Did you already eat breakfast?

B: Yes, I ate breakfast at 6:45.

- Did you already eat breakfast?
- Did you break your pencil last week?
- Did you already know your teacher on the first day of school?
- Did you give someone a present last month?
- Where did you find something you lost?
- When did you have your last birthday party?

134

Grammar Check ✓

Name some **irregular verbs** and their past form.

Writing

Respond to Text

Ongoing
Writing
Skills
Practice

After you read a text, you can write a response. In a response, you say what you think about the text.

Writing Prompt

Write your response to the text *Scientists and Crows*. Be sure to use the simple past of irregular verbs correctly.

❶ Prewrite

Think about the selection *Scientists and Crows*. Complete a chart with what you knew before you read the article, what you found interesting about it, and what surprised you. List your ideas in a three-column chart.

A student named Christina listed her ideas like this:

Crows		
What I Knew	**What I Found Interesting**	**What I Learned that surprised me**
Crows break things apart with their beaks.	Crows figure out ways to break things open.	Crows figured out how to make hooks.

❷ Draft

Use your three-column chart to help you write a first draft.

• Keep in mind your purpose—to write your response to the text.

• Include what you found interesting and what you learned.

❸ Revise

Reread your draft. Look for places where it needs improvement. Use the Writing Checklist to help you find problems. Then revise your draft.

❹ Edit

Check your work for errors. Use the Peer Review Checklist on page 402 .

❺ Publish

Make a clean copy of your final draft. Share it with the class. Save your work. You will need it for the Writing Workshop.

Here is Christina's reaction to the text:

Writing Checklist

Ideas

✓ I included what interested me about the text and what surprised me.

✓ I expressed my ideas clearly.

Conventions

✓ I used the simple past of irregular verbs correctly.

✓ Nouns and pronouns agree.

Christina Ramos

I thought the article <u>Scientists and Crows</u> was very interesting. I knew that crows could break things apart with their sharp beaks, but I didn't know they could break apart things in different ways. For example, they fly high and drop things in the street so cars will break them apart. It surprised me that the crows in the experiment in Japan bent the wire into hooks so they could get the food. Amazing!

WB
135–136

What You Will Learn

Reading
- Vocabulary building: *Context, phonics*
- Reading strategy: *Ask questions*
- Text type: *Informational text (photo essay)*

Grammar
Nouns: common and proper

Writing
Explain a process

These words will help you understand the reading.

Key Words

costume

robe

painting

teepee

mask

quilt

Key Words

In *A Story to Tell*, you will learn about objects Native Americans have made.

Words in Context Audio

1 Joey wore a lion costume in the class play.

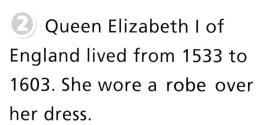

2 Queen Elizabeth I of England lived from 1533 to 1603. She wore a robe over her dress.

3 This artist stands on a ladder to work on his large painting.

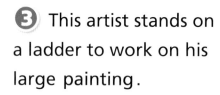

4 A teepee is a kind of tent. Some Native Americans made teepees. They used poles and the skins of animals.

5 A Japanese actor wears this mask to play a young woman.

6 My grandmother made a quilt using different pieces of cloth. It shows a little town.

Practice

Draw pictures of the key words in your notebook. Label the pictures using sentences that contain the key words.

Make Connections

Have you ever made a mask? What did you use to make it? Describe a mask you would like to make. Tell where you would wear it.

These words will help you talk about the reading.

Academic Words

imply
say something in an indirect way

symbol
something that stands for an idea

Academic Words

Words in Context

My teacher told us to review the chapter this weekend. I think he was trying to **imply** there will be a test on Monday.

She uses the sun in her paintings as a **symbol** of happiness.

Practice

Write the sentences in your notebook. Choose an academic word to complete each sentence.

1. The bald eagle is a ____ of freedom in the United States.

2. She talks a lot about nature in her poetry. Her words ____ she cares about the Earth.

Apply

Ask and answer with a partner.

1. What is a **symbol** of happiness to you?

2. What words can you use to **imply** that you like something, without using the word *like*?

Phonics

Hard and Soft c

A **hard c** sounds like the *k* in *kite*. *Classroom* has a **hard c.**

A **soft c** sounds like the *s* in *sun*. *Center* has a **soft c.**

> My seat is in the center of my classroom.

Rule

The letter *c* is soft when it is followed by *e, i,* or *y*.
The letter *c* is hard when followed by *a, o,* or *u*.

Practice

Work with a partner. Take turns.

- Read the sentences aloud.
- List the words with a soft c sound.
- List the words with a hard c sound.

1. An artist carved this mask. He cut into the wood.

2. The dance is part of a celebration.

3. The gardens add color to our city.

4. I drew circles and cubes with my pencil.

WB
139

More About

How do the things people make show their ideas?

 Listen to the Audio.
Listen for the main points and important details.

Reading Strategy

Ask Questions

As you read, ask yourself questions to make sure you understand what you are reading.

- Read the captions and look at the photographs.
- Ask yourself what story each object tells.

Listen as your teacher models the reading strategy.

A Story to Tell

by Cindy Luecke

How do you catch a dream? You need a dream catcher. A dream catcher is just one of the many beautiful **objects** made by Native Americans who lived in parts of the Americas.

Native Americans made things they needed. They made clothing and costumes. They created paintings and **pottery**. All of the objects show what was important to the people who made them. Many of the objects have a story to tell.

---

objects   things you can touch or see

pottery   objects made out of baked clay

The Kickapoo women often made cornhusk dolls for their daughters. The dolls were made of all natural materials that could be chewed on. As the dolls naturally fell apart, it showed that the child was growing up. Many of the dolls were made with hair from their mother's head.

The Maya people act out events that are part of their history. The man is wearing a costume to celebrate the Fiesta de Santo Tomás. The festival is celebrated in Chichicastenango, Guatemala.

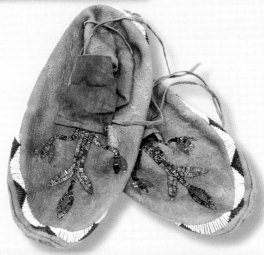

The Hasinai were part of the Caddo **confederacy**. They were also known as *Tejas*, from a word in their language that means *those who are friends*. They made these special kind of shoes called *moccasins*.

This photo shows pictures on a teepee. There are buffaloes and geometric designs.

---

confederacy   A group that includes other groups within it

Before You Go On   A cornhusk doll falls apart. What is the doll a **symbol** of?

An artist **carved** this mask from stone. It is about 600 years old.

Lakota people made this dream catcher using string, beads, and feathers. Lakota legends say that Spider Woman made the first dream catcher. She told them that the web would catch bad dreams and keep them away.

One of the Sioux people wore this warm robe. Notice the painting of riders and horses on the robe. The painting tells us that horses and **warriors** were important to the Sioux.

A Navajo artist creates a colorful sand painting. He uses black, blue, white, and red sand. For hundreds of years, the Navajo have made sand paintings.

---

carved   cut a pattern on a surface

This hand-made **quilt** is in a Native American Seminole pattern. Many Seminoles live in Florida.

Artists use **looms** like this one to **weave** rugs. This artist is using blue, red, and white yarn.

---

looms   frames or machines used to weave on

weave   make threads into cloth

140–142

Reading Strategy

Ask Questions

- What questions did you ask yourself as you read?
- What story did each object tell?
- How did asking questions help you understand the selection?

Think It Over

1. **Recall**   Name three objects that Native Americans have created.

2. **Comprehend**   What images appear in these objects?

3. **Analyze**   Many of the objects are both artistic and practical. What does this **imply** about the people who made them?

Learning Strategies

Ask Questions

As you read, ask yourself questions. This will help you make sure you understand what you are reading. Try these steps.

- Read part of the selection.

- Look at the key words.

- Look at the pictures for clues.

- Ask yourself questions.

- Use what you already know to help you answer the questions.

Practice

Read this passage. In your notebook, list three questions you could ask to be sure you understand it.

> Artists worked together to create this quilt. Each person made one of the squares. The finished work is called a gathering quilt. *Gathering* means *bringing together*.

1. _____

2. _____

3. _____

Use a T-Chart

Use a T-Chart to help make sure you understand what you are reading.

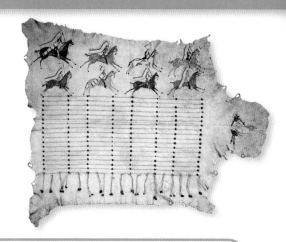

Read this passage from the selection.

> One of the Sioux people wore this warm robe. Notice the painting of riders and horses on the robe. The painting tells us that horses and warriors were important to the Sioux.

- Copy the T-Chart. Fill in how to find the answer to number 3.
- Add your own question. Tell how you can answer it.

Question	How to Find the Answers
1. What was important to the Sioux?	I could reread the passage.
2. What is a robe?	I could look back at the key words page.
3. What other objects did the Sioux make?	

Apply

Summarize the selection for a partner. Use some of the key words as you speak.

143

Extension

Utilize You have learned about some of the beautiful objects that Native Americans have made. Which object described in the selection do you like best? Draw a picture of it. Present your drawing to the class.

Grammar

Nouns: Common and Proper

A **proper noun** names a specific person, place, or thing.
Proper nouns begin with a capital letter. A **common noun**
names a person, place, or thing, but it is not specific.
Common nouns do not begin with a capital letter.
Review the chart:

Catagory	Common Nouns	Proper Nouns
People	a boy a woman	Pablo Mary Smith
Places and Locations	a state a river	South Dakota the Rio Grande
Titles	my doctor my teacher	Dr. Morgan Mrs. Garcia
Relationships	my aunt my uncle	Aunt Rocio Uncle José
Time Periods	last year the ninties	the Middle Ages the Iron Age
Ethnic or National Groups	the tribe the people	Apaches Americans

Practice

Choose the correct word or words. Write the sentences.

Example: Did your (Mother, mother) make these dolls?

Did your mother make these dolls?

1. They are made in (oaxaca, Oaxaca).

2. Does (uncle Joe, Uncle Joe) make pottery?

3. A (navajo, Navajo) artist created this sand painting.

4. I learned about baskets from (dr. Ortiz, Dr. Ortiz).

5. The Caddo Indians made (moccasins, Moccasins).

Apply

Write your answers to the questions. Use common and proper nouns in your answers. Then ask and answer the questions with a partner.

Example: A: Who is our teacher?

B: Our teacher is Mrs. McCoy.

- Who is our teacher?
- What are the names of two classmates?
- What is your mother's name?
- What street do you live on?
- Where were you born?
- What country would you like to visit?
- What do you call your aunt or uncle?

W B
144

Grammar Check ✓

Name a **common noun** and a **proper noun**. Use each one in a sentence.

Writing

Explain a Process

Ongoing Writing Skills Practice

When you write, your ideas must be well organized. This is especially important when you are explaining a process.

Writing Prompt

Write a paragraph explaining a process. Include details about steps and materials. Be sure to use common and proper nouns correctly.

❶ Prewrite [G.O. 144]

Choose something that you know how to make or do. Think about the steps. List your ideas in a Sequence Chart.

A student named Adam listed his ideas like this:

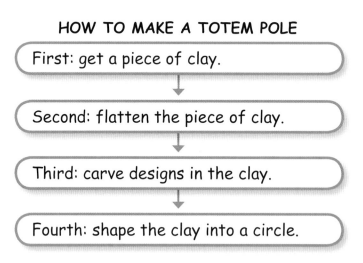

HOW TO MAKE A TOTEM POLE

First: get a piece of clay.

Second: flatten the piece of clay.

Third: carve designs in the clay.

Fourth: shape the clay into a circle.

❷ Draft

Use your Sequence Chart to help you write a first draft.

- Keep in mind your purpose—to explain a process.
- Include all the steps and materials.

❸ Revise

Read your draft. Look for places where the writing needs improvement. Use the Writing Checklist to help you find problems. Then revise your draft.

❹ Edit

Check your work for errors. Use the Peer Review Checklist on page 402.

❺ Publish

Make a clean copy of your final draft. Share it with the class. Save your work. You will need it for the Writing Workshop.

Here is Adam's explanation of how to make a totem pole:

Adam Jensen

I'm learning how to make totem poles in art class. Totem poles were made on the Northwest Coast of the United States. Native Americans made them to tell stories. Here's how I make one:

First, I flatten a piece of clay with my hand. Next, I make designs in the clay with carving tools. Finally, I curve the flat piece of clay into a tube. Now I have a totem pole!

Writing Checklist

Organization

✓ I included all the steps in the correct sequence.

✓ I mentioned what materials I used.

Conventions

✓ I used common and proper nouns correctly.

✓ I used sequence words correctly.

WB
145–146

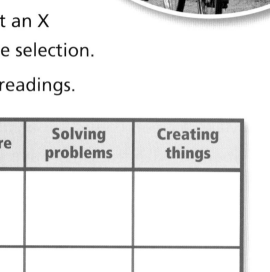

PUT IT ALL TOGETHER

Apply and Extend

Link the Readings

Copy the chart into your notebook. Read the words in the top row.

- For *On Your Bike, Get Set, Donate*!, put an X under the words that remind you of the selection.

- Repeat the same activity for the other readings.

	Informational text	Literature	Solving problems	Creating things
On Your Bike, Get Set, Donate!				
Scientists and Crows				
A Story to Tell				

Discussion

1. In the selection *On Your Bike, Get Set, Donate!*, how do volunteers help people in need?

2. How do the scientists in the selection *Scientists and Crows* test their **theory** about crows?

3. How do the objects described in *A Story to Tell* help us learn more about the Native Americans?

Listening Skills

If you don't understand a word or phrase, you can say, "What does that mean?"

THE BIG QUESTION What are some great ideas that make our world a better place?

Projects

Your teacher will help you choose one of these projects.

Written	Oral	Visual/Active
Invent It	**Show and Tell**	**Robes**
Think of a new invention. Describe what it might look like and what it could do. You may also want to include a labeled diagram.	Think about something important that you use every day. How does it help you? Show and tell why it is important you.	You saw a picture of a Sioux robe. Draw a robe. Then draw pictures on the robe to show things that make your world a better place.
Poem	**Group Plan**	**Mime**
A good poem can start with just one idea. Think of a great idea you want to share. Write about it in a poem.	Work with a group. Talk about ways to help some younger children. Choose one idea. Make a plan. Explain it to the class.	Think of some great inventions. Choose one and act out how to use it. Your classmates must guess what it is.

Further Reading

 For more projects visit
LongmanCornerstone.com

**Tom Thumb**

This Penguin Young Reader® tells the story of how a very small boy uses his tiny size to solve big problems.

Boxes for Katje, Candace Fleming

Katje lives in Holland. After World War II, she gets boxes of supplies from her American pen pal. Katje shares the gifts with her community, and they find a special way to thank their new friend.

147–148

Listening and Speaking Workshop

Give a Presentation

You are going to write and give a presentation. Then you will listen as your classmates give their presentations.

❶ Prepare

A. Choose a favorite hobby or interest you have. You will describe your hobby or interest and explain why you like it. Then your classmates will ask questions about your presentation.

B. Think about what you want to tell your classmates. What is the main idea? What are the details? Find photos, posters, or other props to show during your presentation.

> I like science and space. And I'm going to talk about exploring the night sky. It's my favorite hobby.
>
> I read about different stars and planets and constellations. Then I try to find them with my telescope. This is my telescope. And this is my "Star List". I always keep a list of what I find. Last year, I found 10 stars, 5 planets, and 12 constellations.

❷ Practice

Practice your presentation with your props. Practice in front of your family or friends. If possible, record your presentation. Then listen to yourself. How do you sound? Record yourself again and try to improve.

❸ Present

As you speak, do the following:
- Speak clearly and loudly.
- Show your props.
- After your presentation, answer your classmates' questions.

As you listen, do the following:
- Look at the speaker's props. They will help you understand what you hear.
- Think of questions to ask the speaker after the presentation.

❹ Evaluate

After you speak, answer these questions:
- ✓ Did you describe your hobby or interest clearly?
- ✓ Did you explain why you like it?

After you listen, answer these questions:
- ✓ Was the presentation formal or informal?
- ✓ Think about the general meaning of the presentation. Can you think of a title for it? Tell your idea to the class.

Speaking Skills

Presentations can use formal or informal language. Choose which to use based on your audience and the purpose of your presentation.

Listening Skills

Listen carefully for the speaker's main points and important details. Retell these ideas in your own words to confirm that you have understood them.

Writing Workshop

Write to Compare and Contrast

Writing Prompt

Write an essay comparing and contrasting two people, things, or places. Describe similarities and differences. Group them in a logical order. Use a Venn Diagram for your comparison. Use transition words, like *although* and *however*.

❶ Prewrite

Review the writing you have done in this unit. Then choose two people, things, or places to compare and contrast. List your points in a Venn Diagram.

A student named Angelina decided to compare and contrast herself with the character Fern from the book *Charlotte's Web.* Angelina listed her ideas like this:

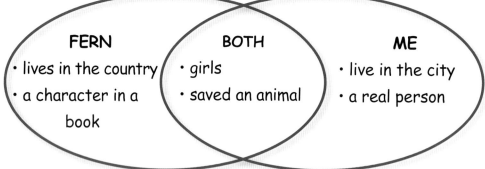

FERN
• lives in the country
• a character in a book

BOTH
• girls
• saved an animal

ME
• live in the city
• a real person

❷ Draft

Use your Venn Diagram to help you write a first draft.

• Keep in mind your purpose—to compare and contrast.

• Include specific details about similarities and differences.

❸ Revise

Read your draft. Look for places where the writing needs improvement. Use the Writing Checklist to help you find problems. Then revise your draft.

Here is how Angelina revised her essay:

Six Traits of Writing Checklist

✔ **Ideas**
Did I explain the similarities and differences between the two subjects?

✔ **Organization**
Did I organize the essay into paragraphs, grouping similarities and differences in a logical order?

✔ **Voice**
Is the voice energetic, lively, and informative?

✔ **Word Choice**
Did I use transition words like *although* and *however*, to show similarities and differences?

✔ **Sentence Fluency**
A variety of sentence lengths and patterns?

✔ **Conventions**
Does my writing follow the rules of grammar, punctuation, usage, and mechanics?

Angelina Castro

The character Fern, from the book "Charlotte's Web," is a girl like me. Although there are some things that are different between us, there ~~is~~ *are* also some important similarities.

Revised to correct verb agreement error.

Fern ~~growed~~ *grew* up on a farm and she is a character in a book but I am a real person.

Revised to correct spelling error

However, in very important ways, Fern and I are both alike. She saved Wilber, the pig. I found my dog, Midnight, at the animal shelter. No one wanted him.

Fern and I are alike in one very important way. We *both* love our special pets!

Revised to make meaning clearer.

4 Edit

Check your work for errors. Trade papers with a partner to get feedback. Use the Peer Review Checklist.

5 Publish

Make a clean copy of your final draft. Share it with the class.

149–150

Peer Review Checklist

✔ The essay is informative.

✔ All the information is related to the topic.

✔ Transition words are used to compare and contrast.

SPELLING TIP

Simple past regular verbs end in *-ed*. But irregular past tense verbs, like *grew* and *found*, don't follow regular spelling patterns. The only way to learn them is to memorize them.

Listen to the sentences. Pay attention to the groups of words. Read aloud.

1. Many volunteer groups fix up old bicycles to donate to other people.

2. Scientists want to find out if crows use instinct or tools to solve problems.

3. Many kinds of art tell stories from different cultures.

Work in pairs. Take turns reading the passage below aloud for one minute. Count the number of words you read.

A Story to Tell describes some of the objects different	10
Native Americans make that tell different stories. The	18
objects play an important part in the history, customs,	27
and needs of peoples' day-to-day life. For example, the	38
Comanche and Caddo Indians made beautiful clothes,	45
boots, and moccasins. In California, native people made	53
baskets with stories of animals. The Lakota people made	62
dream catchers with string, beads, and feathers. Navajo	70
artists made colorful sand paintings. Other peoples carved	78
images into rock or made wooden masks.	85

With your partner, find the words that slowed you down.

- Practice saying each word and then say the sentence each word is in.

- Then take turns reading the text again. Count the number of words you read.

151–152

Test Preparation

Taking Tests

You will often take tests that help show what you know. Follow these tips to improve your test-taking skills.

Coaching Corner

Answering Questions That Have Pictures or Graphics

- Many test questions come with pictures or graphics.
- Before reading the selection, look at the graphic. Make sure you know what it is about.
- Next, read the questions and answer choices.
- Then read any text that comes with it.
- After you read the selection, read the questions. Look at the graphic or picture again.
- Then choose the best answer.
- Check to make sure your answer choices make sense.

Read the following test sample. Study the tips in the box.

153–154

Read the selection and diagram. Then answer the questions.

The First Lady's Garden

The First Lady loves gardens. She even has a garden at the White House. In the spring, the First Lady asked some kids to help her plant a garden. Many kids from local schools came to help. They worked for hours. The First Lady and the kids planted vegetables and herbs. Soon, there were many good things to eat! The White House chef uses the food from the garden.

Main Idea: _____		
Detail There are vegetables, berries, and herbs.	**Detail** Kids helped the First Lady plant the garden.	**Detail** The President's family _____ food from the garden.

1 The main idea is —

  A how kids can eat better.
  B the White House chef.
  C how to eat broccoli.
  D the White House garden.

2 Who helped the First Lady?

  F The President
  G Kids from local schools
  H The White House chef
  J Members of Congress

3 Which word belongs on the blank in the last detail?

  A eats
  B sleeps
  C drives
  D hates

Tips

✓ Be careful. Make sure you know the difference between a main idea and details.

✓ You can almost always get rid of answers that don't make sense. Which answers don't make sense?

Neighbors in Space

The sun, moon,
stars, and planets are Earth's
neighbors in space.

Reading

1 Science

Earth and Beyond

2 Myths

**One Moon,
Many Myths**

3 Biography

Franklin's Dream

Listening and Speaking

You will talk about stars, planets, and astronauts. In the Listening and Speaking Workshop, you will present a TV newscast.

Writing

You will practice persuasive writing. In the Writing Workshop, you will write a review.

Quick Write

Why does the moon change size and shape? Write what you think.

DVD **VIEW AND RESPOND**
Talk about the poster for this unit. Then watch and listen to the video and answer the questions at <u>LongmanCornerstone.com</u>.

What do you know about space?

Words to Know

Listen and repeat. Use these words to talk about space.

 Earth

 moon

 sun

 stars

Practice

Work with a partner. Ask and answer questions.

during the day	at night	both day and night

Example: A: When do you see _stars_?

B: I see _stars_ at _night_.

Write

Read the questions. Write your answers in your notebook.

What do you see in the sky at night? What do you see in the sky during the day?

Make Connections

Copy the sentences into your notebook. Fill in the blanks.

1. I'm made of rock. Sometimes I look round and sometimes I look like only part of a circle. You can see me at night and often during the day. What am I? ____
   a. the sun   **b.** the moon   **c.** the stars

2. I am very hot and very bright. You can hurt your eyes if you look at me. You can see me only during the day. Who am I? ____
   a. the sun   **b.** the moon   **c.** the stars

3. You can see us only at night. There are millions of us. We are very bright, like your sun, but we are very far away. Who are we? ____
   a. the sun   **b.** the moon   **c.** the stars

What about you?

Talk with a partner. Astronauts train to travel to and work in space. Would you like to be an astronaut? Why or why not?

Kids' Stories from around the World

Audio

Philippines

Rodel

We have star parties here in the Philippines. We go to the best places to see the stars. People bring telescopes. We look at the moon and planets, too. Some people take pictures of the night sky.

Fiona

When I grow up, I want to be an astronaut. I just came back from Space Camp in Alabama. There, we learned how it feels to travel in space. We trained like real astronauts. We got to eat space food. We even met an astronaut!

England

Alabama, U.S.A.

Chile

Margaret

I live in England, near Stonehenge. Stonehenge is a large circle of very big stones that was made about 5,000 years ago. No one knows how it was built. Some scientists think people used Stonehenge to mark changes in the sun and moon. It may have been a kind of calendar.

Luis

I live in Chile. One of the biggest telescopes in the world is here. It is called the Very Large Telescope, or VLT. It is four large telescopes that can work together. The VLT is on a high mountain in the desert.

What about you?

1. Do you know a lot about space? If yes, how did you learn? If no, do you want to learn more?

2. Do you have a story about Earth's neighbors in space? Share your story.

What You Will Learn

Reading

- Vocabulary building: *Context, word study*

- Reading strategy: *Use prior knowledge*

- Text type: *Informational text (science)*

Grammar

Compound sentences (*and* and *but*)

Writing

Write a persuasive paragraph

These words will help you understand the reading.

Key Words

- **sphere**
- **craters**
- **billions**
- **planets**
- **rotates**
- **continents**

Key Words

Earth and Beyond tells about the Earth, moon, sun, and stars.

Words in Context

1 The teacher holds a blue sphere in one hand. It is a globe. It shows what Earth looks like.

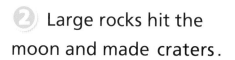

2 Large rocks hit the moon and made craters.

3 How many grains of sand are on a beach? Billions!

4 Earth is one of eight **planets** in our solar system. All eight planets travel around the sun.

5 Earth **rotates**, or turns, on its **axis** as it travels around the sun.

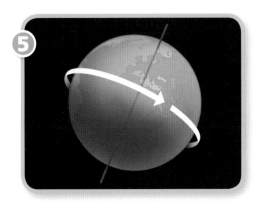

6 Do you recognize these **continents**? Which one is Australia? Which one is Africa? Which one is South America?

[Practice]

Add a page to your vocabulary notebook.
- Divide your page into three columns: the new words, their definitions, and drawings of the words when possible.
- Test yourself by covering one of the columns.

Make Connections

Some people say they feel small when they look at the stars. How do you feel when you look at the night sky? What does it make you think about?

155–156

These words will help you talk about the reading.

Academic Words

assign
give a duty or task

consist of
be made up of

Academic Words

Words in Context Audio

Teachers often **assign** homework to students.

Stars are giant balls in the sky that **consist of** hot gas.

Practice

Write the sentences in your notebook. Choose an academic word to complete each sentence.

1. A story _____ three main parts: plot, character, and setting.

2. Our parents _____ each of us chores to do on Saturdays.

Ask and answer with a partner.

1. What chores at home would you like to **assign** to someone else?

2. A diet is the food you regularly eat. What kinds of foods does your usual diet **consist of**?

Word Study

Synonyms and Antonyms

Synonyms are words that mean the same thing.
(earth—world)

Antonyms are words that have opposite meanings.
(big—small)

Practice

Work with a partner. Choose a synonym or an antonym for each underlined word.

Synonyms

sphere   large   surface

1. Earth is a <u>big</u> ball in space.

2. Like Earth, the moon is a <u>ball</u>.

3. The <u>outside</u> of the moon is dusty.

Antonyms

cold   bright   night

4. Look up at the <u>day</u> sky.

5. The sun is very <u>dim</u>.

6. The temperature on the moon can be very <u>hot</u>.

157

More About

THE BIG QUESTION

What can we learn about Earth and its neighbors?

Listen to the Audio. Listen for the main points and important details.

Reading Strategy

Use Prior Knowledge

Think about what you already know about a topic. This can prepare you to learn more. Before you read, ask yourself:

- What do I already know?
- What do I want to find out?

Listen as your teacher models the reading strategy.

Earth and Beyond

by Maya Hightower
illustrated by Johnnee Bee

We live on Earth. Earth is a sphere. It is a large, round ball in space. But Earth is not alone.

Look up at the night sky. What do you want to learn? What are stars made of? Do people live on the moon?

Look up at the sky in the day. What do you want to learn? How big is the sun? Why can't you see stars during the day?

The more you look, the more questions you will have. Let's travel through space to find some answers.

What do we know about the moon?

The moon is our nearest neighbor in space. It is 239,000 miles (384,833 kilometers) from Earth.

The moon is a sphere, like Earth. The surface of the moon is dusty. It has mountains and plains. Many craters cover the moon's **surface**.

Do people live on the moon?

No! The moon does not have air. The **temperature** can change from very hot to very cold. No plants, animals, or people can live on the moon.

Have people ever visited the moon?

Yes! Twelve **astronauts** have walked on the moon. They wore special suits so they could breathe. They brought back moon rocks.

---

surface   top or outside

temperature   measure of how hot or cold something is

astronaut   someone who travels and works in space

Reading Skill

Ask your classmates or your teacher if you don't understand a word, phrase, or language structure.

Before You Go On   Why can't people live on the moon?

What are stars?

Stars look like tiny lights in the sky, but they are giant balls of hot gas.

How many stars are there?

There are billions of stars in space, but we can't see all of them. On a clear night, we can see thousands of stars.

Why do stars look so small?

Stars look small because they are so far away.

What is a constellation?

A constellation is a group of stars that looks like a picture. Long ago, people looked up at the night sky. They saw shapes made by the stars. People named these shapes for things they knew, such as animals.

What is the sun?

The sun is a star. Earth and the other planets **orbit** the sun.

Why does the sun look so big and bright?

It looks big and bright because it is closer than any other star. The sun is so bright that we can't see other stars during the day.

The sun is always glowing. So why is the sky dark at night?

Earth rotates every 24 hours. When our side of Earth faces the sun, we have day. When our side faces away from the sun, we have night.

Why is the sun so important?

The sun warms and lights Earth.

Can people visit the sun?

No! The sun is too hot.

---

orbit   travel in a circle in space around a larger object

Before You Go On   How did people **assign** names to constellations?

What is the solar system?

The solar system is like a large neighborhood. It is made up of the sun and all the things that orbit the sun. Earth and its moon are part of the solar system. So are other planets and their moons. The solar system also has billions of **asteroids** and **meteors**.

What is a planet?

A planet is a large sphere that rotates in space as it orbits the sun. Some planets are made of rock, and others are made of gas. Some have rings around them, and some have many moons.

What are the planets in the solar system?

Mercury, Venus, Earth, Mars, Jupiter, Saturn, Uranus, and Neptune are the planets.

---

asteroids   small, rocky objects that move around the sun

meteors   pieces of rock or metal that float in space

What is special about the planet Earth?

Earth has water and air. It is the only planet where people, animals, and plants can live.

What does Earth look like from space?

Earth looks like a beautiful ball with many colors. From space, the oceans look blue and the continents look brown and green.

158–160

Reading Strategy

Use Prior Knowledge

- What did you already know before you read?
- What did you want to find out?
- How did thinking about these questions help you understand the selection?

Think It Over

1. **Recall** What does the solar system **consist** of?

2. **Comprehend** What causes day and night?

3. **Analyze** Many objects in space share the same shape. What is it?

Learning Strategies

The 5W Questions

Before you read, think about your purpose for reading. Often we read because we want to learn something. You can help yourself learn more effectively by asking yourself questions that begin with these words:

Who? What? Where? When? Why?

These questions are sometimes called the 5Ws. They focus on people, events, time, places, and reasons.

Practice

With a partner, read *Earth and Beyond* again. Look for answers to the following questions.

1. Who has visited the moon?

2. What does the surface of the moon look like?

3. Where are the moon's craters located?

4. When is it daytime? When is it nighttime?

5. Why can't we see stars during the day?

Use a KWL Chart

What did you already know about space? What did you want to learn? A KWL Chart can help you see what you have learned.

Copy the chart. Complete all three columns. Share your work with a partner.

What I Know	What I Want to Know	What I Learned
I know the moon is in the night sky.	Do people live on the moon?	1. No. There is no air on the moon. 2. No plants, animals, or people can live there.

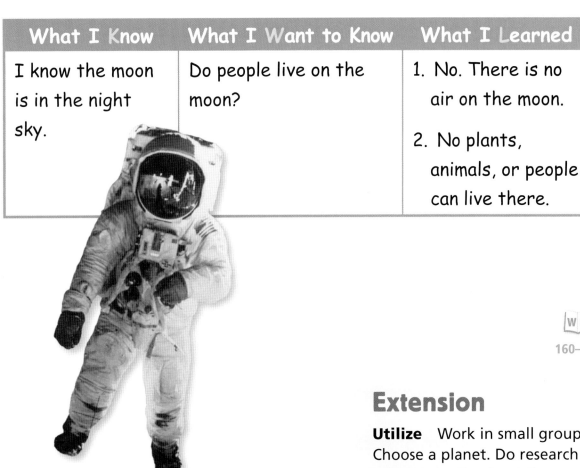

WB
160–161

Extension

Utilize Work in small groups. Choose a planet. Do research independently about the planet your group has chosen. Share your information with your group. Then create a poster together. Share it with the class.

Apply

Summarize the selection. Use some of the key words as you speak.

Grammar

Compound Sentences

A **simple sentence** shows one complete thought:

> Earth's oceans look blue.

A **compound sentence** is made up of two **simple sentences**. Join the simple sentences with a **comma** and a **connecting word**, such as *and* or *but*.

> Earth's oceans look blue. **(+)** The continents look brown.
> Earth's oceans look blue, and the continents look brown.

Use *and* to simply **add** another complete thought. Use *but* to show a **contrast** or **difference** between two complete thoughts.

Simple Sentence	(+)	Simple Sentence
There are billions of stars in space.		We can't see all of them.

↓

Compound Sentence
There are billions of stars in space, *but* we can't see all of them.

A **comma** goes **before** the connecting word in a compound sentence. The comma shows the end of the first complete thought.

Practice

Join each pair of sentences to make a compound sentence. Use *and* or *but*.

Example: It was cloudy. I saw some stars.

It was cloudy, but I saw some stars.

1. Stars look so tiny in the sky. There are so many stars!

2. The sun warms Earth. The sun also gives us light.

3. Some planets have rings around them. Others do not.

4. People saw images in the constellations. They didn't always see the same images.

Apply

Work with a partner. Ask and answer the questions. Use compound sentences.

Example: A: How did you get to school today, and how will you get home?

B: I rode the bus to school, and I'll ride the bus home, too.

162

- How did you get to school today, and how will you get home?
- Where did you eat breakfast yesterday, and where did you eat lunch?
- What time do you wake up on Mondays, and what time do you wake up on Saturdays?
- What subject do you like, and what subject do you *really* like?

Grammar Check ✓

Write a **compound sentence** using *and* or *but*.

Writing

Write a Persuasive Paragraph

Ongoing Writing Skills Practice

In a persuasive paragraph, your goal is to persuade the reader to agree with you.

Writing Prompt

Write a persuasive paragraph about whether you think learning about space is important. Be sure to use compound sentences, and to use the connecting words *and* and *but* correctly.

❶ Prewrite G.O. 141

Decide whether you think learning about space is important. List the ideas that support your belief in a chart.

A student named Kim listed her ideas like this:

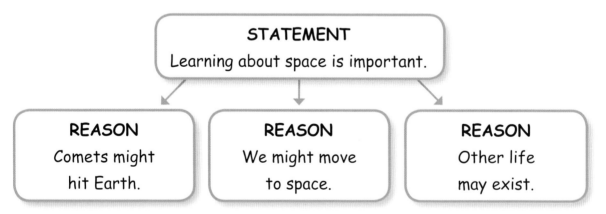

STATEMENT
Learning about space is important.

REASON
Comets might hit Earth.

REASON
We might move to space.

REASON
Other life may exist.

❷ Draft

Use your chart to help you write a first draft.

- Keep in mind your purpose—to persuade the reader.
- Include reasons for your belief.

❸ Revise

Reread your draft. Look for places where it needs improvement. Use the Writing Checklist to help you find problems. Then revise your draft.

❹ Edit

Check your work for errors. Use the Peer Review Checklist on page 402.

❺ Publish

Make a clean copy of your final draft. Share it with the class. Save your work for the Writing Workshop.

Here is Kim's persuasive paragraph:

Kim Yang

Learning about space is important. There are many reasons why. First, scientists need to know if a comet is going to hit the Earth and when. Second, the number of people on the Earth is growing too large. We may have to move to another planet someday. Third, it is important to find out if life forms exist on other planets. Space exploration is expensive, but it is a benefit to everyone.

WB

163–164

Key Words

What You Will Learn

Reading
- Vocabulary building: *Context, word study*
- Reading strategy: *Compare and contrast*
- Text type: *Literature (myths)*

Grammar
Future: *be going to*

Writing
Write a prediction

These words will help you understand the reading.

Key Words

bark

rainbow

canoe

handprints

In *One Moon, Many Myths*, you will read different myths about the moon.

Words in Context

❶ The bark of a tree is its outer covering. Different trees have different kinds of bark.

❷ You can see a rainbow when the sun shines through drops of water. This can happen in the sky. It can also happen close to you.

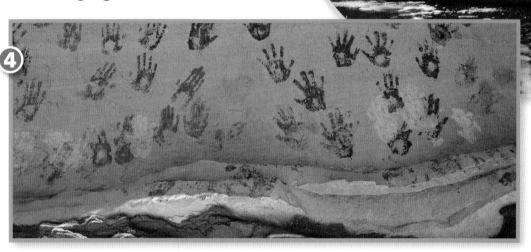

3 This family paddles a canoe. They wear life jackets to be safe.

4 Native Americans made these handprints on a cave wall long ago.

___Practice___

Draw pictures of the key words. Label each picture with a sentence that contains the key word.

Make Connections

What do you look at in nature? Do you look at the bark on trees? Have you ever seen a rainbow? Describe what you like to look at when you are outside.

165

These words will help you talk about the reading.

Academic Words

Academic Words

phenomenon
something we can observe, or see

traditional
following ideas or methods that have existed for a long time

Academic Words

Words in Context Audio

Sometimes a **phenomenon** is uncommon, such a double rainbow.

My grandfather makes a **traditional** dessert that his mother made when he was little.

Practice

Write the sentences in your notebook. Choose an academic word to complete each sentence.

1. The northern lights are a natural ____. They sometimes appear in the night sky.

2. My aunt wears a hanbok, which is a ____ Korean dress, to our family celebrations.

Apply

Ask and answer with a partner.

1. Which natural **phenomenon** is the most frightening? A tornado, a hurricane, or an earthquake? Why do you think so?

2. What **traditional** events does your town have in the summer or during the holidays? Describe them.

Word Study

Multiple-Meaning Words

Some words have more than one meaning, such as the word *bark.*

1. The bark on this tree is brown.

2. Look at the dog bark!

> **bark¹** outer covering of a tree
> **bark²** make a short, loud sound

Practice

Work with a partner. Read each sentence.

Choose the best meaning for the underlined word.

1. Last night I <u>saw</u> a full moon.

> **saw¹** looked at
> **saw²** a tool with a sharp blade

2. It's not raining hard. It's only raining a little <u>bit</u>.

> **bit¹** took a bite of
> **bit²** small amount

167

LITERATURE
Myths

More About

Why did people make up stories to explain things in space?

 Listen to the Audio.
Listen for the main points and important details.

Reading Strategy

Compare and Contrast

Comparing and contrasting helps you to understand ideas in a text.

- To compare, look for ways the myths are the same.
- To contrast, look for ways the myths are different.

Listen as your teacher models the reading strategy.

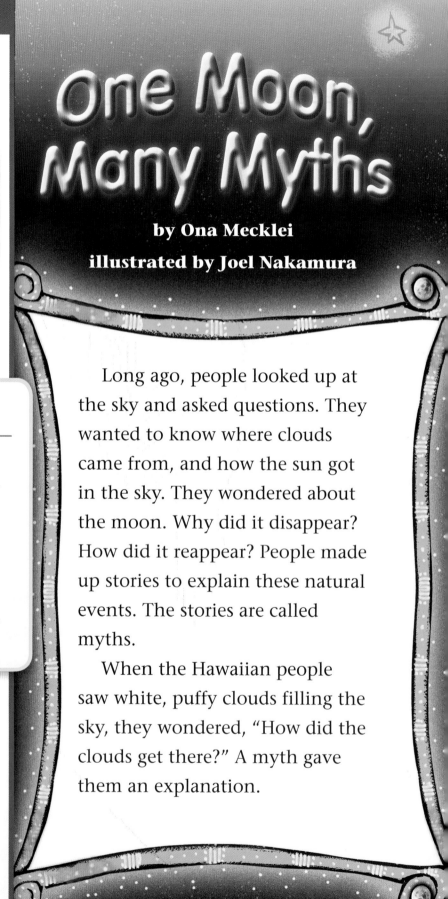

One Moon, Many Myths

by Ona Mecklei

illustrated by Joel Nakamura

Long ago, people looked up at the sky and asked questions. They wanted to know where clouds came from, and how the sun got in the sky. They wondered about the moon. Why did it disappear? How did it reappear? People made up stories to explain these natural events. The stories are called myths.

When the Hawaiian people saw white, puffy clouds filling the sky, they wondered, "How did the clouds get there?" A myth gave them an explanation.

Hina and the Moon

Long ago, people made cloth from bark. They beat the bark, and it became soft cloth.

Hina lived on Earth long ago. One night, she saw a full moon. A rainbow stretched from the moon to Earth.

"I will climb to the moon," she said. And she did.

Hina began to beat bark. The cloth was white. She threw her cloth over Earth. The cloth became a cloud.

Hina is still on the moon to this day, making clouds.

Before You Go On What **traditional** task does Hina perform while she is on the moon?

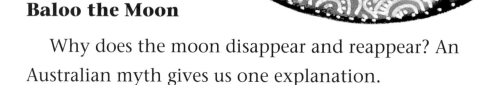

Baloo the Moon

Why does the moon disappear and reappear? An Australian myth gives us one explanation.

Baloo the Moon came to Earth. He saw two girls in a canoe. He tried to step into the canoe, but…splash! Baloo fell into the water! When the girls in the canoe saw this, they started to laugh.

Baloo was **embarrassed**, so he hid himself in the sky. Then, after a little time had passed, he began to show a bit of his face. Then he showed more of his face. Finally, Baloo showed his whole face. But then he remembered how the girls had laughed, so he hid his face again.

Baloo does this again and again. That is why the moon disappears and reappears.

---

embarrassed   ashamed in front of others

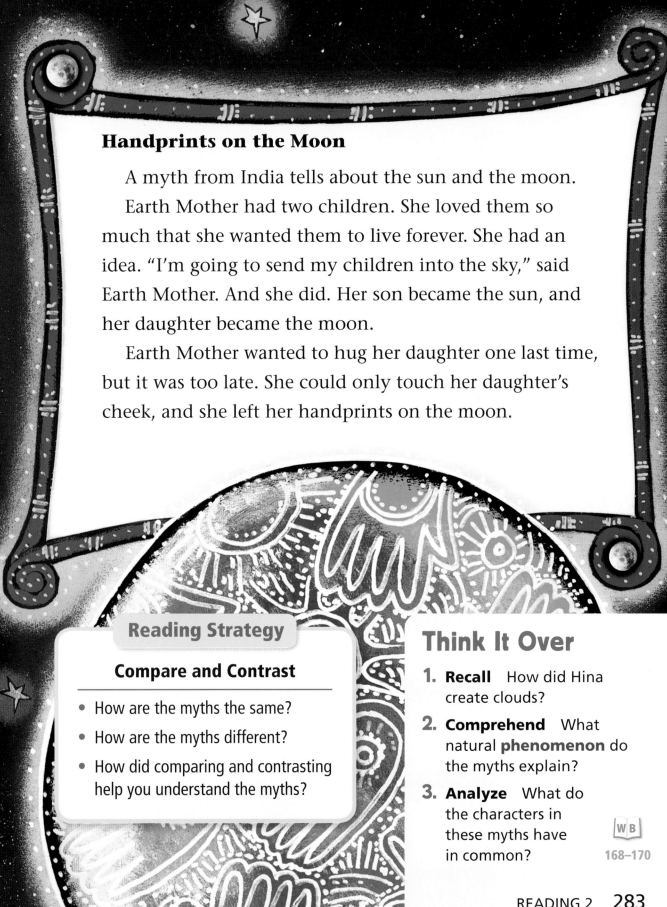

Handprints on the Moon

A myth from India tells about the sun and the moon.
Earth Mother had two children. She loved them so
much that she wanted them to live forever. She had an
idea. "I'm going to send my children into the sky," said
Earth Mother. And she did. Her son became the sun, and
her daughter became the moon.

Earth Mother wanted to hug her daughter one last time,
but it was too late. She could only touch her daughter's
cheek, and she left her handprints on the moon.

Reading Strategy

Compare and Contrast

- How are the myths the same?
- How are the myths different?
- How did comparing and contrasting help you understand the myths?

Think It Over

1. **Recall** How did Hina create clouds?

2. **Comprehend** What natural **phenomenon** do the myths explain?

3. **Analyze** What do the characters in these myths have in common?

WB

168–170

Learning Strategies

Compare and Contrast

When you **compare** things, you tell how they are alike.
When you **contrast** things, you tell how they are different.

Practice

Read these sentences about the selection. Tell whether the sentences compare or contrast the myths.

1. All three myths tell about things in the sky.

2. Characters in all the myths do impossible things.

3. Hina climbs to the moon on a rainbow. Baloo the moon comes to Earth. Earth Mother's children become the sun and moon.

4. All three myths explain something in nature.

5. Hina makes the clouds. Baloo makes the moon appear and disappear. Earth Mother made handprints on the moon.

Use a Venn Diagram

A Venn Diagram can help you compare and contrast. The outside of the circles tells what is different. The part where the circles link tells what is alike.

Copy and complete the diagram.

1. Compare and contrast the two myths.

2. Make another Venn Diagram. Compare and contrast the Indian myth with the Baloo myth or the Hina myth.

BALOO MYTH   **HINA MYTH**

1. Tells why the moon disappears and appears again
2. Comes from Australia
3. _____

1. Explains something in nature
2. Tells about things in the sky
3. _____

1. Tells where clouds come from
2. Comes from Hawaii
3. _____

W|B
171

Apply

Retell the selection to a partner.

Extension

Utilize   Create a myth that tells why there are so many stars in the sky. Share your myth with the class.

Grammar

Future: *be going to*

To talk about the future, you can use *be going to* or *will*.

> "I'm **going to** send my children into the sky," said Earth Mother.
> "I **will** climb to the moon," Hina said.

The *be going to* form is used more frequently than *will.* Use *be going to* to talk about plans and predictions. Be sure the *be* verb agrees with the subject.

> They're **going to have** a study group. (a plan)
> I'm **going to be** the president someday. (a prediction)

To make a negative sentence with *be going to,* use *not* between the *be* verb and *going to.*

> I'm **not going to watch** that show.
> She **isn't going to close** the window.
> They **aren't going to come** to our play.

To make questions with *be going to,* put the *be* verb before the subject.

> **Is** he **going to read** the story aloud?
> When **are** we **going to have** our next exam?

Practice

Change the verb in each sentence to show the future. Write the sentences.

Example: We talked about the moon.

We are going to talk about the moon.

1. The teacher did not ask questions.

2. She reads books to us.

3. Alana saw a movie with her friends.

4. I did my science homework in the library.

5. My mom doesn't read this magazine.

Apply

Work with a partner. Ask and answer the questions. Use the future with *be going to* in your answers.

Example: A: Are you going walk home after school?

B: Yes, I'm going to walk home after school.

- Are you going to walk home after school?
- Is your family going to watch television tonight?
- Are you going to study later?
- Are you going to call anyone?
- Are you going to do anything this weekend?
- Are you going to bring your lunch tomorrow?

Grammar Check ✓

Write a sentence using the **future with *be going to***.

Writing

Ongoing Writing Skills Practice

Write a Prediction

A prediction is a statement about what you think is going to happen. To make a prediction persuasive, support it with reasons.

Writing Prompt

Write a prediction about where you think the United States is going to travel in space next. Give reasons to support your prediction. Be sure to use *be going to* correctly.

❶ Prewrite

Decide where you think the United States is going to travel next in space. List reasons to support your prediction in a graphic organizer.

A student named Kaisha listed her ideas like this:

> **PREDICTION**
> I predict that the United States is going to explore the moon again.

> **REASON**
> We learned that there is water on the moon.

> **REASON**
> We can use the moon as a station.

❷ Draft

Use your graphic organizer to help you write a first draft.

- Keep in mind your purpose—to make a prediction.

- Include reasons that support your prediction.

❸ Revise

Reread your draft. Look for places where it needs improvement. Use the Writing Checklist to help you find problems. Then revise your draft.

❹ Edit

Check your work for errors. Do Peer Review (use the Checklist on page 402).

❺ Publish

Make a clean copy of your final draft. Share it with the class. Save your work. You will need it for the Writing Workshop.

Here is Kaisha's paragraph:

Writing Checklist

Ideas

✔ I stated my prediction clearly.

✔ I listed reasons that support my prediction.

Conventions

✔ I used *be going to* correctly.

✔ Subjects and verbs agree.

Kaisha Okar

I predict that the United States is going to explore the Moon again. There are several things that make the Moon important for scientists. Scientists learned recently that there is water on the Moon. There could be enough water to fill a reservoir in Europe. Also, scientists can use the Moon as a station on the way to other planets. This is why I think the United States is going to return to the Moon.

WB 173–174

What You Will Learn

Reading
- Vocabulary building: *Context, phonics*
- Reading strategy: *Summarize*
- Text type: *Informational text (biography)*

Grammar
Complex sentences: *because* and *so*

Writing
Write a persuasive letter

These words will help you understand the reading.

Key Words

- **space shuttle**
- **flight**
- **satellite**
- **observe**
- **spacewalks**

Key Words

Franklin's Dream tells about a boy who grew up to become an astronaut.

Words in Context Audio

1 Astronauts ride a space shuttle to go into space and come back to Earth. A trip in space is called a space flight.

2 The space shuttle may take a satellite into space. A satellite orbits Earth. Satellites help telephones and televisions work.

3 Scientists **observe** the stars through a telescope.

4 Astronauts take **spacewalks** to go outside the space shuttle.

Practice

Make flashcards to help you memorize the words.
- Write a key word on the front.
- On the back, write the meaning.

Make Connections

Would you like to be an astronaut?
Why or why not?

These words will help you talk about the reading.

Academic Words

immigrate
enter another country in order to live there

significant
important

Academic Words

Words in Context

Some people **immigrate** to another country to find a better way of life.

The invention of the cell phone has had a **significant** affect on how we communicate with each other.

Practice

Write the sentences in your notebook. Choose an academic word to complete each sentence.

1. There is a _____ difference between my old school, which was small, and my new school, which is large.

2. My grandparents _____ to the United States when my mother was a baby.

Apply

Ask and answer with a partner.

1. If you could choose another country to live in, which country would you **immigrate** to? Why?

2. What **significant** events have happened in your school this year?

Phonics

R-Controlled Vowels: *ar, or, ore*

The letter *r* changes vowel sounds. Listen. Then read each word aloud.

am	ton	toe
arm	torn	tore

Rule

The letters *ar* usually have the vowel sound heard in **art**. The letters *or* and *ore* usually have the vowel sound heard in **born** and **more**.

Practice

Read the sentences with a partner. Take turns.

- Read the sentences aloud. Listen for words that have r-controlled vowels.
- List the words with *ar*.
- List the words with *or* and *ore*.

1. His story starts in Costa Rica.

2. That is where he was born.

3. He was a smart child.

4. He enjoyed sports.

5. He wanted to explore space.

177

More About

How can someone become an astronaut?

 Listen to the Audio.
Listen for the main points and important details.

Reading Strategy

Summarize

Summarizing a selection helps you check that you understood what you read.

• Think about what is important in the selection.

• Identify the main idea.

• Identify the important details.

Listen as your teacher models the reading strategy.

Franklin's Dream

by Mirna Cepeda
illustrated by Nathan Hale

It is 1986. The space shuttle *Columbia* lifts off. Franklin Chang-Diaz is on the shuttle. This is his first space flight. His dream has come true.

Franklin was born in San José, Costa Rica. When he was a boy, he heard about *Sputnik*. *Sputnik* was the first satellite to orbit Earth.

Franklin climbed a mango tree. He watched the sky for hours.

"I was seven years old," he said, "when I decided to become an astronaut."

Franklin never let go of his dream.

Before You Go On   What **significant** event caused Franklin to want to become an astronaut?

Franklin was a good student in school. But that was not all. He was a **curious** child. He liked to observe the things around him. He tried to learn more about them. Sports and music were his hobbies. Science and reading were the **subjects** he liked best. He planned to study science.

curious   wanting to know or learn things

subjects   main things you study in school

Reading Skill

If you don't understand something, ask your classmates or your teacher, "What does this mean?" If you think you understand but you want to make sure, ask, "Does this mean…?"

Franklin liked to repair things. He found out how they worked. Then he tried to make them work better.

Franklin hoped to become an astronaut. He knew that a good education would help him. He also knew that he needed to learn English. So he moved to the United States. His parents helped him.

Franklin kept working hard. He learned English, and he studied science. His teachers helped him. He went to **college**. Franklin became a **scientist**.

---

college school after high school

scientist someone who works in science

Before You Go On   Why did Franklin and his family **immigrate** to the United States?

In 1980, Franklin was chosen to become an astronaut. He started to train in classrooms and in labs. After six years of training, he was ready. It was 1986, the year of *Columbia's* flight.

Franklin flew on a total of seven space flights—more flights than anyone had ever gone on before. He would later become a director at Johnson Space Center in Houston. He **retired** from **NASA** in 2005.

These days, Franklin is the **CEO** of a **rocket** technology company, and a professor of physics at Rice University and the University of Houston.

---

retired   stopped working

NASA   National Aeronautics and Space Administration

CEO   Chief Executive Officer

rocket   a space vehicle

Flying in space is exciting. But for Franklin, the sight of Earth from outer space is the best part. He says that it is very beautiful. He says that we must take care of Earth.

"Earth is **humanity's** spaceship and the only one we have," says Franklin. "We must protect it."

----

humanity's belonging to all people

Reading Strategy

Summarize

- What was the main idea of the selection?
- What were the important details?

Think It Over

1. **Recall** Where was Franklin born?

2. **Comprehend** Describe Franklin. What was he like as a boy? Give details.

3. **Analyze** How does his experience as an astronaut help him on his current jobs?

Space Exploration

▲ Blast off!
A space shuttle begins its flight into space.

▲ Docking
Astronauts ride the space shuttle to get to the space station. The space shuttle docks, or links, to the space station.

▲ Spacewalk
An astronaut goes on a spacewalk to work outside the space shuttle.

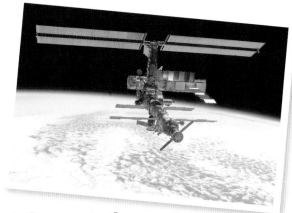

▲ Space station
This is the International Space Station. People from many countries work here.

▲ Red planet

A robot took this picture of the surface of Mars. Mars is often called the red planet. Can you tell why?

▲ Robot on Mars

People have not walked on Mars—yet! But scientists sent this robot there. The robot helped scientists study rocks.

◀ Moon walk

Buzz Aldrin was an astronaut on the first trip to the moon in 1969.

Activity to Do

These two pages use words and pictures to tell about space exploration.

- Choose another type of exploration
- Find pictures to show that exploration.
- Post your pictures and captions in your classroom.

Learning Strategies

Summarize

To **summarize**, tell only the main idea and the most important details.

Practice

Read these details from the selection. Choose three important details.

1. Franklin was born in Costa Rica.

2. Franklin climbed a mango tree.

3. Franklin moved to the United States and learned English.

4. Franklin's hobbies were sports and music.

5. Franklin worked hard in school. He became a scientist.

6. Flying in space is exciting.

7. Franklin flew on more space flights than anyone had flown before.

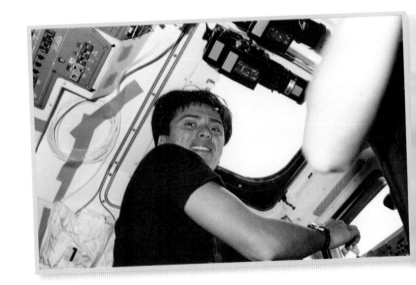

Use a Main Idea and Details Chart

A Main Idea and Details Chart can help you summarize what you read.

Copy the chart into your notebook.

> **MAIN IDEA**
> Franklin's dream was to become an astronaut.
> He achieved his goal.

DETAIL:	DETAIL:	DETAIL:
Franklin was born in Costa Rica.		

Choose two details that support the main idea.
Add them to the chart.

1. Franklin climbed a mango tree.
2. Franklin worked hard in school. He became a scientist.
3. Franklin flew on more space flights than anyone had flown before.
4. Flying in space is exciting.

Reread the selection and take notes.
Then close your book and retell the selection to a partner.

Extension

Utilize Franklin Chang-Diaz had a dream. Think of a time when you had a special dream. Tell a partner what you did to make your dream come true.

W B

181

Grammar

Complex Sentences: *because* and *so*

A **clause** is a group of words containing a subject and a verb. You can use *because* and *so* to connect clauses. Sentences with *because* and *so* are called *complex sentences.*

Use *because* to give a reason:
> We must take care of the earth because it is the only one we have.

Use *so* to give a result:
> Franklin studied hard so he could become an astronaut.

If the clause with *because* begins the sentence, you should use a comma between the clauses.

Franklin liked to observe things *because* he was curious.
Because he was curious, Franklin liked to observe things.

Practice

Join each pair of sentences to make a
complex sentence. Use *because* or *so*.

Example: I get up early. I can walk my dog.

I get up early so I can walk my dog.

1. I look through a telescope. I can see the stars.

2. Many students work hard. They have a goal.

3. People immigrate. They want to live in that country.

4. I try to repair things. I can learn how they work.

5. Astronauts ride the space shuttle. They want to explore space.

Apply

**Work with a partner. Ask and answer the questions.
Use a complex sentence in your answer.**

Example: A: What sports do you like, and why?

B: I like soccer because I like to run.

182

- What sports do you like, and why?
- Are you interested in space? Why or why not?
- Why are students late for school?
- Why do we sometimes work with a partner?
- Why do many people eat a healthy breakfast?
- What place would you like to visit, and why?

Grammar Check ✓

Write one **compound
sentence** using
because or *so.*

Writing

Write a Persuasive Letter

Ongoing Writing Skills Practice

A persuasive letter is a letter asking someone to help you.

Writing Prompt

Write a business letter to NASA asking them to accept you at their Space Camp. Give reasons to support your request. Be sure to use connecting words and complex sentences correctly.

1 Prewrite

G.O.
152

Decide why you would benefit from Space Camp. List reasons to support your argument in a Three-Column Chart.

A student named Yu-Min listed her ideas like this:

WHY I SHOULD ATTEND SPACE CAMP		
REASON 1	REASON 2	REASON 3
I'm in good physical condition.	I can build a rocket ship model.	I'm very good at math and science.

2 Draft

Use your Three-Column Chart to help you write a first draft.

- Keep in mind your purpose—to persuade NASA to accept you to their Space Camp.
- Include reasons that explain your statement.

❸ Revise

Read your draft. Look for places where it needs improvement. Use the Writing Checklist. Then revise your draft.

❹ Edit

Check your work for errors. Use the Peer Review Checklist on page 402.

❺ Publish

Make a clean copy of your final draft. Share it with the class.

Here is Yu-Min's letter:

Writing Checklist

Ideas

✓ I stated my request clearly.

Organization

✓ I presented my reasons in a logical order.

Conventions

✓ I used connecting words and complex sentences correctly.

183–184

---

554 East 76th Street
New York, NY 10116

NASA Headquarters
Washington DC, USA 20546

December 21, 2010

To whom it may concern:

Please consider me as a candidate for Space Camp. I have many of the same interests and abilities as astronauts. First of all, I'm in very good physical condition. Second, I could help build a space ship because I have experience building models. Finally, I'm very good at math and science. They are my favorite subjects.

Sincerely,
Yu-Min Lee

PUT IT ALL TOGETHER

Apply and Extend

Link the Readings

Copy the chart into your notebook. Read the words in the top row.

- For *Earth and Beyond,* put an X under the words that remind you of the selection.

- Repeat the same activity for the other readings.

	Informational text	Literature	The moon	Science
Earth and Beyond				
One Moon, Many Myths				
Franklin's Dream				

Discussion

1. What interests and significant events in Franklin's life prepared him to become an astronaut?

2. What objects in space do the three myths talk about?

3. How is *Earth and Beyond* similar to *One Moon, Many Myths?*

 What can we know about our neighbors in space?

> **Listening Skills**
>
> If you don't understand something, you can say, "I don't understand. Can you explain, please?"

Projects

Your teacher will help you choose one of these projects.

Written	Oral	Visual/Active
Space Story	**Space Facts**	**Moon Map**
Write a story about a trip to a planet. Tell what the planet is like. Tell what happens to the astronauts who go to that planet.	List three facts about one of Earth's neighbors in space. Read your facts aloud. Have a partner guess which neighbor goes with your list.	Find a map of the moon on the Internet. Make a model of the moon. Make labels to show the craters and seas on the moon.
Planet Song	**Biography Lesson**	**Space Mobile**
Write a song about the planets. Name all the planets. The song should help you learn the order of the planets from the sun.	Pick an astronaut besides Franklin Chang-Diaz. Find out about that astronaut's trip into space. Tell what he or she has done in space.	Make a mobile of our solar system. On the back of each picture, write a fact about it. Hang the mobile in your classroom.

Further Reading

For more projects visit
LongmanCornerstone.com

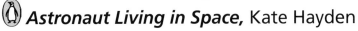

Astronaut Living in Space, Kate Hayden

Find out what it's like to be an astronaut! Follow astronaut Linda Gardner as she prepares for a flight into space, and then as she experiences the actual flight.

Draw Me a Star, Eric Carle

A young boy draws a star. He keeps drawing to fill the world with all kinds of living things. Years later, he draws another star for the moon and it takes him across the night sky.

185–186

Listening and Speaking Workshop

Present a TV Newscast

You are going to write and present a TV newscast. Then you will listen as your classmates present their newscasts.

❶ Prepare

A. Find a partner. Decide on a story about space or space exploration. You will present this story.

B. Each of you will describe a part of the story. Find props or other visuals to use during your newscast.

News Anchor 1:	I'm Sam Yee. Here's an interesting story. NASA's dog, Jupiter, landed on Mars this morning.
News Anchor 2:	I'm Tonya Vasquez. And that is interesting, Sam. But here's something truly amazing. At the exact time Jupiter landed on Mars, a dog on Earth named Tiny ran into its front yard and started to jump into the air and bark.
News Anchor 1:	Does anyone know why Tiny did this?

❷ Practice

Practice your TV newscast in front of your family or friends. As you work together, listen to each other's ideas and work cooperatively.

❸ Present

As you speak, do the following:

- Face your audience.
- Speak clearly and loudly.
- Show your props or other visuals.

As you listen, do the following:

- Take notes about *Who*? *What*? *When*? *Where*? and *How*?
- Listen carefully for ideas and information that is not stated directly.
- Pay close attention. Your teacher will ask you questions after the newscast.

❹ Evaluate

After you speak, answer these questions:

- ✓ Did your group give details and other important information about the news story?
- ✓ Did your group use formal language?

After you listen, answer these questions:

- ✓ Did the newscasters speak clearly and directly to the audience?
- ✓ Did the newscasters use formal language?

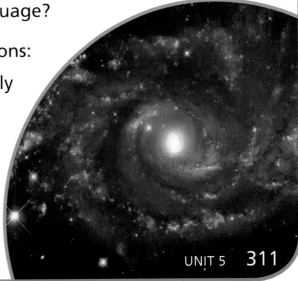

Writing Workshop

Write a Book or Movie Review

Writing Prompt

Write a movie or book review. Include details about the characters, plot, and setting. List this information in a graphic organizer.

❶ Prewrite

Review the writing you have done in this unit. Now choose a movie or book to review. What is your opinion of it? How can you persuade the reader of your review to agree with you? List your points in a graphic organizer. A student named Kevin listed his ideas like this:

> **Title:** The Christmas Rat
>
> **Author:** Avi
>
> **My opinion:** A fantastic book!
>
> **Setting:** The action takes place in Eric's basement.
>
> **Characters:** Eric and the exterminator, Anje.
>
> **Plot:** A fight between Eric and Anje about a rat in the basement.

❷ Draft

Use your graphic organizer to help you write a first draft.

- Keep in mind your purpose—to write a book review.
- Include details that will persuade the reader to agree with your opinion.

❸ Revise

Read your draft. Look for places where the writing needs improvement. Use the Writing Checklist to help you find problems. Then revise your draft.

Here is how Kevin revised his essay.

Six Traits of Writing Checklist

✓ **Ideas**
Do I give reasons to support my opinion?

✓ **Organization**
Are my supporting reasons organized into paragraphs?

✓ **Voice**
Is my voice informative and persuasive?

✓ **Word Choice**
Did I use a variety of adjectives?

✓ **Sentence Fluency**
Did I use a variety of sentence lengths and patterns?

✓ **Conventions**
Does my writing follow the rules of grammar, punctuation, usage, and mechanics?

Kevin Zheng

The Christmas Rat by Avi is a very suspenceful mystery.

> **Revised** to correct spelling error.

The setting of this story is mostly in the basement. The basement is dark and creepy. The story is dark and creepy, too, so the basement is a good place for the setting.

The story's characters and plot are complex and interesting. Eric is a lonely 9-year-old boy. At first he want to help the exterminator, Anje, kill a rat that lives in the basement. Eric slowly realizes that he doesn't want to help Anje, but Anje is unhappy about Eric's change in attitude. Could Eric be in danger?

> **Revised** to correct verb agreement error.

> **Revised** to make meaning clearer.

Read The Christmas Rat soon. You'll love it!

❹ Edit

Check your work for errors. Trade papers with a partner to get feedback. Use the Peer Review Checklist on page 00. Edit your final draft in response to feedback from your partner and your teacher.

❺ Publish

Make a clean copy of your final draft. Share it with the class.

187–188

Peer Review Checklist

✓ The introduction states the author's opinion.

✓ The ideas and opinions expressed are clear.

✓ The supporting reasons are convincing.

SPELLING TIP

Pay attention to words ending in -*se* and -*ce*. American English and British English have different rules about these spellings, so it is common for writers to get them mixed up. You have to memorize how these words are spelled.

Listen to the sentences. Pay attention to the groups of words. Read aloud.

1. Some of our neighbors in space are the moon, the sun, stars, and planets.

2. Many different stories explain the behavior of objects in the sky.

3. Franklin Chang-Diaz's dream to become a NASA astronaut came true.

Work in pairs. Take turns reading the text below aloud for one minute. Count the number of words you read.

Franklin's Dream tells the story of a little boy who wanted	11
to fly into space. He moved with his parents from his home in	24
Costa Rica to the United States. He studied hard, learned English,	35
and became a scientist. In 1980, he was chosen by NASA to	47
become an astronaut. After six years of training, he had his first	59
flight on the space shuttle Columbia. His dream came true.	69
Franklin flew on seven space flights. After his flights, he	79
became a director at Johnson Space Center in Houston. He	89
retired from NASA in 2005. Now he is a physics professor.	100

With your partner, find the words that slowed you down.

- Practice saying each word and then say the sentence each word is in.

- Then take turns reading the text again. Count the number of words you read.

189

Test Preparation

Taking Tests

You will often take tests that help show what you know. Follow these tips to improve your test-taking skills.

Coaching Corner

Answering Questions About a Selection

- Many test questions ask you to answer questions about a selection.

- The selection can be fiction or nonfiction.

- The selection can be long or short.

- Before you read the selection, preview the questions and answer choices.

- After reading the selection, first try to answer each question in your head.

- Choose the answer that comes closest to the answer in your head.

- Check to make sure your answer choice is supported by the text.

Read the following test sample. Study the tips in the box.

191–192

Read the selection. Then answer the questions.

July 20, 1969, was the first day a man walked on the moon. The mission was called Apollo 11. Three astronauts traveled in a spaceship to reach the moon. They were Neil Armstrong, Michael Collins, and Edwin "Buzz" Aldrin. The main spaceship was the Columbia. It had a smaller ship inside. The smaller ship was the Eagle. The Eagle landed on the moon. Neil and Buzz walked on the moon. At the same time, Michael orbited the moon in the Columbia. When they all came back to Earth, they got a hero's welcome.

1 What was the name of the mission?

  A Apollo 11
  B Columbia
  C Eagle
  D Apollo 13

2 How many astronauts walked on the moon?

  F One
  G Two
  H Three
  J Four

3 Which is the best summary of this paragraph?

  A The life of Neil Armstrong
  B The day man first landed on the moon
  C The making of Apollo 11
  D Returning home to a hero's welcome

Tips

✓ Be careful. Two of the answer choices in Question 1 have the same word. The other two answer choices are also in the selection. Only one answer is correct.

✓ Make sure the answer you choose makes sense.

Arts Festivals

People have arts festivals to celebrate the fun of making and sharing art.

Reading

1 | Social Studies

Arts Festival!

2 | Instructions

How to Make Puppets

3 | Article

Bonnaroo Music and Arts Festival

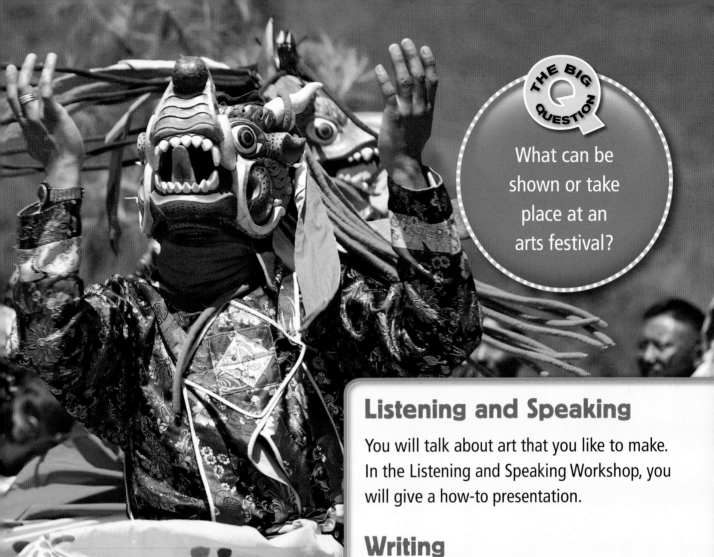

What can be shown or take place at an arts festival?

Listening and Speaking

You will talk about art that you like to make. In the Listening and Speaking Workshop, you will give a how-to presentation.

Writing

You will practice skills needed to write a research report. In the Writing Workshop, you will write a research report.

Quick Write

Look at the picture of the puppets. Tell how you would make a puppet.

DVD

VIEW AND RESPOND

Talk about the poster for this unit. Then watch and listen to the video and answer the questions at LongmanCornerstone.com.

What do you know about art?

Words to Know

Listen and repeat. Use these words to talk about art.

 puppets

 mask

 paper flowers

 mural

 vase

Work with a partner. Ask and answer questions. Try to extend your conversation.

A: Do you know how to make <u>puppets</u>?

B: No, I don't. Do you?

A: Yes, I do. I made <u>puppets</u> once in Mr. Kelly's class.

Read the question. Write your response in your notebook.

Write two or three sentences about a piece of art you have in your home or your classroom. What does it look like?

Make Connections

Copy the conversations into your notebook. Complete the sentences.

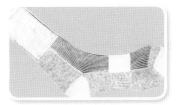
a sock

tissue paper

paintbrushes

paints

1. **A:** Look. I found this old ____ in my room.

   B: You should use it to make a puppet.

2. **A:** Let's paint our masks now.

   B: OK. I have paint, but we need two ____.

3. **A:** What can I make for my mom for her birthday?

   B: Let's use this ____ to make some paper flowers.

4. **A:** What happens if you mix black and white ____ ?

   B: The color becomes gray.

What about you?

Talk with a partner. Describe how you make a craft. Then, listen to your partner. Can you follow his or her directions?

Kids' Stories from around the World

Audio

Mongolia

Oyon

Here in Mongolia, we think horses are very important. We have horse races. We also celebrate horses in art. For the Rainbow Horse Festival, artists made 88 horse sculptures. Children painted the horse sculptures. It was a great festival.

Stacey

There is a big storytelling festival where I live in Tennessee. People come from all over to tell stories. The storytellers make us laugh. They tell tales about the past. Children can also tell stories at the festival.

Ireland

Tennessee, U.S.A.

Anguilla

Aidan

I live in Galway, Ireland. There is an arts festival for children. We go to see musicians, actors, and dancers. Then they teach us how to be artists, too! At the festival, my sister learned to play an Irish drum.

Ben

I live in Anguilla, in the Caribbean Sea. We have an arts festival. Artists from around the world show their paintings. There is a contest for the best one. The winner's picture is put on a postage stamp.

What about you?

1. What kind of art do you like to make or see?

2. Do you have a story about an arts festival? Share your story.

Prepare to Read

What You Will Learn

Reading

- Vocabulary building: *Context, phonics*

- Reading strategy: *Identify author's purpose*

- Text type: *Informational text*
  - *poster*
  - *schedule*
  - *business letter*

Grammar
Commas

Writing
Plan a research report

These words will help you understand the reading.

Key Words

festival
advertise
schedule
supplies

Arts Festival! tells about a big event in the town of Red Tree.

Words in Context

1 My neighborhood has a Cinco de Mayo festival. It is like a big party. We celebrate our Mexican history. There is delicious food, an art show, and great music.

Class 3-A Morning Schedule

8:30–8:45 Morning Greeting

 8:45–9:30 Science

9:30–10:15 Art

10:15–11:00 Math

11:00–12:00 Reading

12:00–12:45 Lunch

2 This is a poster to advertise a dance festival at a school. People will see the poster and come to the dance festival.

3 This schedule tells what Class 3-A does each morning.

4 Here are some of my school supplies. I have pencils, a pencil sharpener, an eraser, and a ruler.

Practice

Make flashcards to help you memorize the words.
- Write a key word on the front.
- On the back, write the meaning.

Make Connections

What art do you like to make? Do you like to draw, dance, or sing? Tell what you would do at an arts festival.

193

These words will help you talk about the reading.

Academic Words

Academic Words

annual
happening every year

participate
be involved in

Words in Context

Our school has an **annual** election. Every year we choose a new class president.

Sometimes I **participate** in a discussion. Other times I just listen and don't say anything.

Practice

Write the sentences in your notebook. Choose an academic word to complete each sentence.

1. My family always goes to the _____ rodeo in Houston, Texas.

2. If runners want to _____ in the race, they need to arrive early.

Ask and answer with a partner.

1. What is an **annual** event that you look forward to each year?

2. What is your favorite school activity to **participate** in?

WB
194

326   UNIT 6

Phonics

Diphthongs: *ou, ow*

Read the words. Listen for the vowel sounds.
Then read each word aloud.

ou	*ow*
out	how
sound	brown

Rule

The diphthongs *ou* and *ow* have the sound you
hear in **house**.

Practice

Work with a partner. Take turns.

• Read the sentences. Listen for words that
  have diphthongs.

• List words with *ou*.

• List words with *ow*.

• Add three more words to each list.

1. How do you make a puppet?

2. I will use this brown yarn.

3. She drew a mouth on the face.

4. Find out what you can do!

195

More About

Why is it important to
advertise an arts festival?

 Listen to the Audio.
First, listen for the main points.
Then listen again for important
details. Take notes as you listen.

Reading Strategy

**Identify Author's
Purpose**

Authors write for different reasons.
As you read, look for the author's
purpose.

- An author may write to tell
  about something, or to get
  readers to do something.

- An author may write something
  for readers to enjoy.

Listen as your teacher models the
reading strategy.

ARTS FESTIVAL!

by Rouenna Albright

The town of Red Tree has an
arts festival each year. It is called the
Summer Arts Festival. All the people
in the town come.

Children and **adults** can
take art classes. They can go to a
demonstration to learn how to
make pottery or a **collage**.

People work
together to get
ready for the
arts festival. One
person makes
a poster. Another
person makes
a schedule.
Ms. Tan, the art
teacher, writes a letter.

---

adults   fully grown people

demonstration   showing how to do something

collage   picture made by attaching different
pictures onto a surface

Poster

This poster tells about the arts festival. It tells what day the festival is. It tells where the festival will be. The poster helps advertise the festival. People put up posters around Red Tree. Other people will see the posters. They will want to come to the festival.

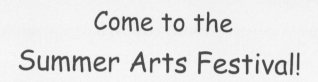

Come to the
Summer Arts Festival!

When? Saturday, June 3, 10 AM
Where? The Middle School Field and Gym
What? Art Activities for All Ages

AND The Great Puppet-Making Contest
Make your own puppet. Win a prize.

Join your friends and neighbors
at the festival.

Before You Go On How does the poster help advertise the festival?

Business Letter

Ms. Tan writes a formal letter. In her letter, Ms. Tan asks for a **donation**.

---

donation   something someone gives

Ms. Jun Tan
Red Tree Arts Center
233 Ferry Road
Red Tree, CA 92688

Ms. Kay Cork
Cork Arts and Crafts
531 South Drive
Red Tree, CA 92688

May 14, 2010

Dear Ms. Cork,
    The Summer Arts Festival will take place in June. This year, there will be a puppet-making contest. Anyone can enter.
    I am writing to ask for your help. We need art supplies for making puppets. We need colored paper, paste, crayons, and markers.
    Many people in Red Tree come to the festival. Your donation would be a great way to advertise the store. It will also help the artists of Red Tree!

Thank you,

Jun Tan
Art Teacher

Schedule of Events

This schedule tells when events will take place.

Summer Arts Festival

10:00   Morning Classes
                Painting
                Drawing
                Crafts

11:00   Pottery Demonstration

12:00   Family Painting Class

1:00   Afternoon Classes
                Painting
                Drawing
                Pottery

2:00   Collage Demonstration

3:00   Puppet-Making Contest

4:00   Art Show
                Prizes for Best Puppets

WB
196–198

Reading Strategy

Identify Author's Purpose

- Think about the poster, schedule, and letter. What was each author's purpose?

- How did looking for the author's purpose help you to understand?

Think It Over

1. **Recall** What is the **annual** arts festival called?

2. **Comprehend** What events can people **participate** in at the arts festival?

3. **Analyze** How do the poster, letter, and schedule contribute to the success of the arts festival?

READING 1   **331**

Learning Strategies

Author's Purpose

Authors have different reasons for writing. Here are ways to find the **author's purpose**.

If the selection . . .		the author's purpose is to
tells about something,	⟶	inform.
tries to get the reader to do something,	⟶	persuade.
is written for the reader to enjoy,	⟶	entertain.

Practice

Think about the parts of *Arts Festival!* Tell if the author's purpose is to inform, persuade, or entertain.

1. The Summer Arts Festival poster
2. The Summer Arts Festival schedule
3. Jun Tan's formal letter

Use a T-Chart

You can use a T-Chart to show the author's purpose.

Copy the T-Chart. Fill in each author's purpose. Then fill in the author's purpose for passages 1, 2, and 3 below.

Selection	Author's Purpose
poster	inform
schedule	
formal letter	
1.	
2.	
3.	

1. Larry hopped into the room. It was his first day. The children looked at him. Some of them laughed. Larry did not care. He was happy to be the first rabbit to take art class.

2. We should have art every day. Then we would have more time to paint. We would also learn more about painting.

3. Painting is an old form of art. People have used paints for more than 20,000 years. The first paintings were in a cave.

199

Summarize the selection for a partner.

Extension

Utilize Reread the passage about Larry (Number 1). Create a story that tells what Larry does in art class. Share it with a partner.

Grammar

Commas

Commas are used to separate words or phrases. Commas can make writing easier to read and understand.

This chart shows some common uses of the comma. Review these rules and examples.

DATES
- between the day of the week and the date:
  Saturday, June 3
- between the date and the year:
  May 14, 2010

LOCATIONS
- between the city and state in addresses:
  531 South Drive
  Red Tree, CA 92688

- between the city and state in sentences:
  I lived in Houston, Texas for two years.

LETTERS
- after the greeting:
  Dear Ms. Cork, / Hi Lola,

- after the closing:
  Thank you, / Sincerely,

SERIES (a series is three or more items)
- between all items:
  We need colored paper, paste, crayons, and markers.

Add commas where they belong. Write the sentences.

Example: He comes from Austin Texas.

He comes from Austin, Texas.

1. He will arrive on Tuesday November 7.

2. I saw Rick Donna and Linda at the party.

3. My cousins live in Galveston Texas.

4. Where were you on May 13 2009?

5. We ate oranges figs grapes and bananas.

 Apply

Work with a partner. First, write your answers to the questions. Make sure to use commas where needed. Then read the questions and answers aloud.

Example: A: What city and state do you live in?

B: I live in Fort Worth, Texas.

- What city and state do you live in?
- What are three things you like to do?
- What are your three favorite television shows?
- What city and state would you like to visit?
- What month, day, and year were you born?
- What are five things you see in our classroom?
- What is today's date?
- What are four foods you like to eat?

200

Grammar Check✓

Write a sentence that includes a **series**. Use **commas** correctly.

Writing

Ongoing Writing Skills Practice

Plan a Research Report

In a research report, you explain a topic that you have studied.

Task 1

First, choose a topic. What interests you? What would you like to learn more about? List a topic in a graphic organizer. Then write some questions and answers about the topic.

A student named Elissa listed her ideas in this chart:

BROAD TOPIC:	Mexican artists
QUESTION:	Who are some famous Mexican artists?
ANSWER:	Frida Kahlo and Diego Rivera.
QUESTION:	Why is Frida Kahlo famous?
ANSWER:	She painted brightly colored pictures with images of her country.

Elissa decided to write her report about her second question, "Why is Frida Kahlo famous?"

Write a Research Question

Next, Elissa made a list of questions about Frida Kahlo.

1. When was Frida Kahlo born?

2. How did Frida Kahlo's life affect her art?

3. What is Frida Kahlo's most famous painting?

Task 2

Study your list of questions. Then choose the question that interests you most. This question will direct the research for your report.

Make a Research Plan

Elissa chose question number 2 as the topic for her report. To create a research plan, she made a list of things she wanted to know about this topic. She listed them in a T-Chart:

What do I want to know?	Where can I find this information?
1. What was Frida Kahlo's early life like?	Website: http://www.girls-explore.com/bios/frida-kahlo.php
2. How did Frida Kahlo feel about her art?	Book: <u>Frida Kahlo</u>, by Jill A. Laidlaw
3. What were Frida Kahlo's paintings like?	Encyclopedia: World Book Encyclopedia, article by Deborah Leveton

Task 3

Create a research plan. Make a list of what you want to learn and where to look for it. Use a T-chart.

Reading 2

Prepare to Read

What You Will Learn

Reading

- Vocabulary building: *Context, phonics*

- Reading strategy: *Identify steps in a process*

- Text type: *Informational Text (instructions)*

Grammar
The imperative

Writing
How to write a paraphrase

These words will help you understand the reading.

Key Words

puppets
scissors
stapler
yarn
buttons

Key Words

How to Make Puppets tells how to make a puppet.

Words in Context

1 Puppets can be big or small. Some you move with strings. Some can fit on your fingers.

2 Some scissors cut paper. Other scissors cut cloth.

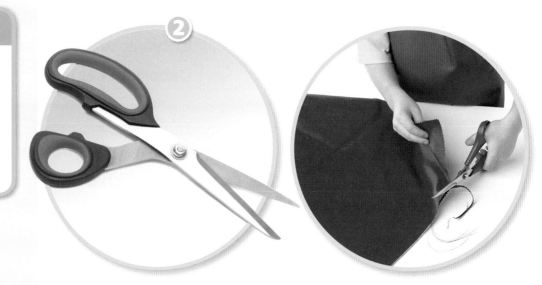

338 UNIT 6

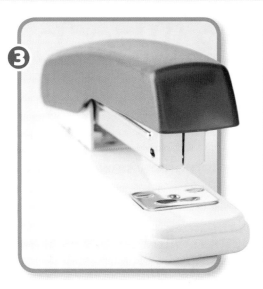

3 A stapler is a useful tool. This boy staples pieces of paper to make a paper chain.

4 They are knitting with yarn. The grandmother helps the girl.

5 Buttons come in many shapes and sizes. Would you like these buttons on a shirt?

Practice

Draw pictures of the key words. Label each picture with a sentence that contains the key word.

Make Connections

Do you like to make crafts? What would you make with yarn, buttons, and cloth?

 WB

203

These words will help you talk about the reading.

Academic Words

Academic Words

required
something needed

reverse
backward; opposite way

Words in Context Audio

All that is **required** for tomorrow's exam is a pencil and an eraser.

When you make a question with *be* you **reverse** the order of the subject and verb.

Practice

Write the sentences in your notebook. Choose an academic word to complete each sentence.

1. Before making a birdhouse, gather together all of the parts that are _____.

2. My brother's name in _____ is M-A-S.

Apply

Ask and answer with a partner.

1. What kind of clothing is **required** for a trip to a very cold place?

2. Can you say the alphabet in **reverse**, starting with *z*? Try it.

WB
204

 Phonics

The Letter Y

The letter *y* can be a vowel. It can be a consonant, too.
Listen. Then read each word aloud.

Vowel: long *e*	Vowel: long *i*	Consonant
city	my	you
party	try	yes

Rule

The letter *y* may have a long *e* sound at the end of the word.
The letter *y* may have a long *i* sound at the end of the word.
The letter *y* may be a consonant when it is at the start of a word or syllable.

Practice

Work with a partner. Take turns.

- Read the words in the chart. Listen for the sounds of the letter *y*.
- Add six words to each list.

WB PH

205

INFORMATIONAL TEXT

Instructions

More About

Why is it important to read directions to make a craft?

Listen to the Audio.
First, listen for the main points. Then listen again for important details. Take notes as you listen.

Reading Strategy

Identify Steps in a Process

Identifying the steps in a process can help you understand how information is connected.

- Look at the pictures.
- Pay attention to the order of the steps for making a puppet.

Listen as your teacher models the reading strategy.

How to Make Puppets

by Pravina Cole

People have been making puppets for thousands of years. Children like to play with puppets. People can use puppets to tell stories, too.

Do you know how to make a puppet? You can learn. Read the directions. First, you need to **gather** the supplies.

---

gather   get things and put them together

What You Will Need

- white paper plates
- scissors
- stapler
- glue
- yarn
- buttons
- colored paper
- crayons, markers, or paint

scissors

paper plates

yarn

stapler

buttons and colored paper

crayons, markers, and paint

glue

Before You Go On | What things are **required** to make this puppet?

1. Staple two paper plates together. The top of the plates should face inside. Do not staple all the way around. Leave a space at the bottom open.

2. With scissors, cut off the bottom part of the top paper plate. This will make a place for you to put your hand.

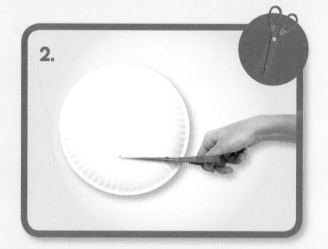

3. Use buttons and colored paper. Use crayons, paint, or markers. Make eyes, a nose, and a mouth for your puppet. Use yarn or paper to make hair or a hat.

4. Now you have made a puppet. Put your hand inside the space between the two paper plates. You can move the puppet by moving your hand.

Can you make your puppet talk? What will it say?

Use your puppet to put on a show or to tell a story.

WB
206–208

Think It Over

1. **Recall** Which step explains how to make the puppet's face?

2. **Comprehend** How do you make a place to hold the puppet?

3. **Analyze** What would happen if you **reversed** the order of steps 1–3? Would the process still work?

Reading Strategy

Identify Steps in a Process

- What are the steps for making a puppet?

- Did identifying the order of the steps help you understand the selection? How?

Puppets

▲ Sock puppet

A sock puppet is easy to make. You just need a clean sock and some buttons.

▲ Puppeteer

The person who works a puppet is a puppeteer. This puppeteer and puppet are in India.

▲ Shadow puppets

This is a shadow puppet show in Malaysia. Can you see the sticks? Puppeteers use the sticks to move the puppets.

▲ Behind the stage

These puppeteers watch their puppets on a video screen. They can see the stage during the show.

▲ Marionette

Marionettes are puppets that hang from strings. When the puppeteer moves the strings, the puppet moves.

▲ Puppets that teach

These puppets help teach children about people with physical challenges. One puppet is in a wheelchair. The other cannot see.

Activity to Do

These two pages use pictures and words to tell about puppets.

- Choose another toy.
- Find pictures to show that toy.
- Post your pictures and captions in your classroom.

Learning Strategies

Reread for Details

If you do not understand the selection the first time you read it, read the selection again. You may also find new information the second time you read it.

Practice

Look back in the selection for the answers to these questions. Tell the page number you found the answer on.

1. What can people use puppets to do?

2. What supplies do you need?

3. After you staple the two paper plates together, what's the next step?

4. When the puppet is finished, how can you move it?

Use a Sequence Chart

To make a puppet, you have to follow the steps in the right order.

 G.O. 144

Complete this Sequence Chart. List the steps given below in the right order.

- Cut off the bottom part of the top paper plate. This will make a place for you to put your hand.

- Place your hand inside the space between the two paper plates. You can move the puppet by moving your hand.

- Staple the paper plates together around the edges. Leave a space at the bottom open.

- Make eyes, a nose, and a mouth for your puppet. Add hair or a hat.

Reread the selection and take notes. Then close your book and retell the selection to a partner.

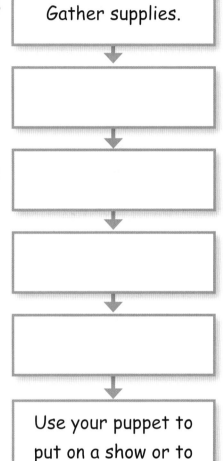

Gather supplies.
Use your puppet to put on a show or to tell a story.

Grammar

The Imperative

We use the **imperative** when we want to tell someone what to do. An imperative sentence usually begins with a verb. The subject "you" is implied.

> Open your books to page 350.

Here are some common ways the imperative form is used:

To give a direct order:
- **Read** the directions.
- **Help** your brother.

To give instructions:
- **Close** your book.
- **Go** upstairs and turn right.

To make an invitation:
- **Come in** and **sit** down.
- **Try** one of these cookies.

To make the imperative sound more polite, add the word please:
- *Please* **stand** up.
- **Open** the window, *please*.

Imperative sentences can also be negative:
- **Don't stay up** too late.
- Please **don't forget** to call.

Practice

Change each question into an imperative. Write the sentences.

Example: Will you make a marionette?

Make a marionette.

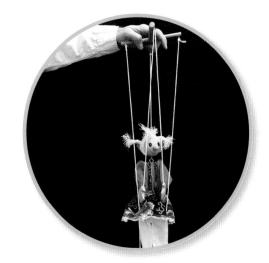

1. Can you sing this song?

2. Will you stand on the stage?

3. Will you hold a microphone?

4. Can you introduce yourself?

5. Will you tell the name of the song?

Apply

Work with a partner. Choose one of the questions below and write instructions. Use imperative sentences. Then tell your instructions to your partner.

Example: A: How do you make a sandwich?

B: First, see what is in the refrigerator. Next,...

- How do you make a sandwich?
- How do you play soccer?
- How do you make a bed?
- How do you make breakfast?
- How do you draw a picture?
- How do you play tag?

210

Grammar Check ✓

Write two **imperative** sentences: one affirmative, and one negative.

Writing

Ongoing Writing Skills Practice

How to Write a Paraphrase

One way to support your ideas in a research report is to put the information you find into your own words. This is called **paraphrasing.**

Task

Find information about an art form, such as photography or painting, or about a favorite artist. Then paraphrase this information in your own words. List your ideas in a graphic organizer. Give information about your source.

A student named Elissa listed her ideas in this chart.

Information from Text
• had polio when she was six • the disease made her right leg weak • in a bus accident when she was 18 • began to paint while in bed
Paraphrase of Information
When she was six, she had polio. This made one of her legs weak. When she was 18, she was in a bad bus accident. She couldn't leave her bed, but she began to paint again.
Research Source
"Frida Kahlo." <u>Girls Explore</u>. 20 December 2010. http://www.girls-explore.com/bios/frida-kahlo.php

Writing Information about a Source

When Elissa wrote her description of her research source, she included the following information:

- the name of the article "Frida Kahlo"
- the name of the website <u>Girls Explore</u>
- the date she found the information (December 20, 2010)
- the address of the website (http://www.girls-explore.com/bios/frida-kahlo.php).

Here is part of Elissa's Research Report. It is based on the paraphrase she wrote.

Elissa Chen

Frida Kahlo had many difficult times in her life. When she was six years old, she became ill with a serious disease called polio. This made one of her legs weaker than the other. When she was 18, she was in a terrible bus accident. It took her a long time to get better. Even though she couldn't leave her bed, she continued to paint.

Works Consulted List

"Frida Kahlo." <u>Girls Explore</u>. 20 December 2010.
   <http:www.girls-explore.com/bios/frida-kahlo.php>

Prepare to Read

What You Will Learn

Reading

- Vocabulary building: *Context, word study*

- Reading strategy: *Draw conclusions*

- Text type: *Informational text (newspaper article)*

Grammar
Quotations

Writing
How to use quotations

These words will help you understand the reading.

Key Words

perform
artists
musicians
instruments
booths

Key Words

The Bonnaroo Music and Arts Festival is about a fun event in Tennessee.

Words in Context Audio

1 Singers **perform** to entertain people and to make money.

2 **Artists** create drawings, paintings, and sculpture as a hobby or as a job.

3 These boys are **musicians** in their high school marching band. They play trumpet and saxophone.

④ The guitar and the drums are typical rock band **instruments**.

⑤ Several **booths** at this outdoor market have plants for sale.

Practice

Add a page to your vocabulary notebook.

- Divide your page into three columns: the new words, their definitions, and drawings of the words when possible.

- Test yourself by covering one of the columns.

Make Connections

Do you like to sing or play an instrument? Which do you like better? Performing on stage, or watching someone else perform?

These words will help you talk about the reading.

Academic Words

alternative
different from something else

goal
something you want to achieve

Academic Words

Words in Context Audio

At home we have many **alternative** activities besides watching TV.

Al's **goal** was to read two more books before the end of summer.

Practice

Write the sentences in your notebook. Choose an academic word to complete each sentence.

1. My _____ for this year is to be on time to all of my classes.

2. The road is closed. We have to find an _____ way to get to the store.

Apply

Ask and answer with a partner.

1. How do you spell and pronounce your name? What is an **alternative** way to spell or pronounce your name?

2. What is one of your **goals** for the next week? What is one of your **goals** for the next 24 hours?

Word Study

Multi-Syllable Words

Read the words in the chart.

1 Syllable	2 Syllables	3 Syllables
jazz	lead/er	af/ter/noon
my	out/door	beau/ti/ful
booths	trum/pet	Sat/ur/day

Rule

Each syllable has one vowel sound. The vowel sound may be spelled with more than one vowel letter.

Practice

Work with a partner. Make a chart with three columns like the one above.

- Write each word below in the correct column.
- Add two new words to each column.

tradition	music	crowd	festival	great
microphone	drum	solo	dancers	

215

Reading 3

INFORMATIONAL TEXT

Newspaper Article

More About THE BIG QUESTION

What could you see and do at the Bonnaroo Music and Arts Festival?

Audio Listen to the Audio.

First, listen for the main points. Then listen again for the important details. Take notes as you listen.

Reading Strategy

Draw Conclusions

To draw a conclusion from what you read, put together details from the selection.

- What activities can people participate in at the festival?
- What do people say about the festival?
- What can you conclude about the people who attend the festival?

Listen as your teacher models the reading strategy.

THE BONNAROO MUSIC AND ARTS FESTIVAL

by C. J. Pallof

The Bonnaroo Music and Arts Festival is held every summer in Manchester, Tennessee. It lasts four days. It is held outdoors. Musicians and bands come from around the world to perform all kinds of music like jazz, country, and rock. A lot of the music has **roots** in American tradition.

---

roots   where something began

Jazz is an African-American **style** of music that began in the southern United States in the early twentieth century. Jazz musicians play many kinds of instruments such as the horn, piano, and guitar.

Country music also began in the South. Country musicians like to play guitars and fiddles.

Rock music began in the mid-twentieth century. It has roots in both jazz and country music. It started in the United States and the United Kingdom. Rock musicians like to play electric guitars and drums.

---

style   the way something is said, done, expressed, or performed

Before You Go On   What kinds of music can people listen to at the festival?

Over 65,000 people attend Bonnaroo. Whole families go because it is fun for adults and kids. There is a tent called Kidz Jam where kids can play musical instruments such as guitars and drums.

But there is more than music at Bonnaroo. There is art, too. Artists show their work in huts called pods. They are made from recycled material such as rubber tires. The artists teach kids how to create art, too. Kids can make a t-shirt or poster of their favorite band.

At the festival's Victory Garden, you can learn to grow your own food. But that's not all. There are games, rides, and a giant ferris wheel that lights up the night. You can also enjoy an outdoor movie at night.

Ginnie Dickinson has gone to the festival many times. "There is so much to do," she said. "And there is new music each year. I love the **folk** music. My daughter Teagan likes rock. We both love to dance!"

---

folk   music that started with common people, not trained musicians

Before You Go On   What **alternative** activities are there for kids besides listening to music?

Splash-a-roo is another fun activity. It is a water park with giant water slides. It is a great way to cool off.

There are also booths where local restaurants sell all kinds of food. You can buy pizza, hamburgers, hotdogs, and more. Or you can cook out in the campground. At night, most people like camping out under the stars at Bonnaroo. There is a special campground just for families, too. It is away from the stages so young children can sleep.

Safety is important at summer festivals. It is easy to get lost in the crowds. And getting sunburned is no fun. Bonnaroo has tents where lost children and adults can find each other. These tents also have sunblock and water. Dancers must drink lots of water to stay cool because Tennessee is very hot in June!

216–218

Reading Strategy

Draw Conclusions

- What can you conclude about the people who come to the festival?
- What details in the selection helped you reach this conclusion?

Think It Over!

1. **Recall** What is the **goal** of the Kidz Jam tent?
2. **Comprehend** What are some ways that people other than musicians contribute to the festival?
3. **Analyze** Why would going to this festival be a fun activity for a family to do together?

Learning Strategies

Draw a Conclusion

To **draw a conclusion**, use details from the selection to make your own ideas. The 5 W questions can help you identify important details. The 5 W questions are *who, what, where, when,* and *why.*

[Practice]

Answer the questions. Draw a conclusion about the reasons people attend the Bonnaroo Music and Arts Festival.

1. Who attends the festival? Children? Adults?

2. Why do people go to the festival? What do you think the main reason is?

3. What does the festival offer to people besides concerts?

4. What are some additional reasons people attend the festival? Explain how you reached this conclusion.

Use a 5 W Chart

Use a 5 W Chart to ask questions about the Bonnaroo Music and Arts Festival.

Copy the chart. Use your answers to draw a conclusion about the music festival.

Who?
_____
_____

What?
_____
_____

Where?
_____
_____

Conclusion
_____
_____

When?
_____
_____
_____

Why?
_____
_____
_____

219

Apply

Summarize the selection. Use some of the key words as you speak.

Extension

Utilize   Work with a partner. Create a dance to your favorite type of music. Perform your dance for the class.

Grammar

Quotations

A **direct quotation** shows a speaker's **exact words**. **Quotation marks (" ")** show a reader where the spoken words begin and end.

> **Direct Quotation showing what David says:**
>
> "I can't wait to go back," says David

Read the following quotations. Notice how a **comma** is used before or after the quotation. Also notice that the first word of a direct quotation is capitalized.

> The guide said, "The festival has a special place just for kids."
> "It's called Kidz Jam," she said.
> "You learn about different instruments," she continued.

Do not add a comma after a quotation if the quotation ends with a question mark or exclamation point:

> "Are there booths with ice cream and dessert?" asked David's father.
> "What a great band!" said David.

Practice

Add quotation marks to show exactly what words the person said. Use commas correctly. Write the sentences.

Example: He said You did great!

He said, "You did great!"

1. I love those musicians said Anita.

2. Me, too! exclaimed her friend.

3. This is a great festival added Tony.

4. Anita said Are all artists this good?

5. My **goal** is to be like them Tony said.

Apply

Work with a partner. Ask and answer the questions. As you talk, write down a few sentences from your conversation. Punctuate each direct quotation.

Example: A: "How old are you?" my partner asked.

B: "I'm eight years old," I replied.

- Do you like music?
- What kind of music do you like?
- Can you play an instrument?
- Who's your favorite singer?
- What's your favorite band?
- How often do you listen to music?
- Do you like to sing?
- Did you ever take dance lessons?

220

Grammar Check ✓

Give an example of a **direct quotation**.

Writing

Ongoing Writing Skills Practice

How to Use Quotations

In addition to paraphrasing, another way to support your ideas in a research report is to use **quotations**. A quote is what other people have said or have written about your topic. You can find quotations for your research report from different sources, including books, magazines, and websites.

After the quotation you must also include information about the source of the quote. Put the author's name or the name of the website in parentheses at the end of the quotation.

Task

Find research information about an art form, such as photography or painting, or about an artist that you like. Include at least one quotation from a research source. Put quotation marks around the words you use. List your ideas in a graphic organizer.

A student named Elissa listed her ideas in this chart:

QUOTATION	"In spite of my long illness, I feel immense joy in LIVING!"
SOURCE	Laidlaw, Jill A. <u>Frida Kahlo</u>. Connecticut: Franklin Watts, 2003.

Writing information about a Source

When Elissa wrote her description of her research source, she included the following information:

- the name of the author (Jill A. Laidlaw)
- the name of the book (<u>Frida Kahlo</u>)
- the location and name of the publisher (Connecticut: Franklin Watts)
- the year the book was published (2003)

Here is part of Elissa's Research Report. It includes the quotation from the book. At the end of the quotation, she included a citation for the quote. The citation is the author of the book's last name and the page number where she found the quote.

> Elissa Chen
>
> Although she suffered many difficulties in her lifetime, Kahlo never lost her love for life. "In spite of my long illness," she said, "I feel immense joy in LIVING." (Laidlaw 39)
>
> **Works Consulted List**
>
> Laidlaw, Jill A. <u>Frida Kahlo</u>. Connecticut: Children's Press, 2003.

Apply and Extend

Link the Readings

Copy the chart into your notebook. Read the words in the top row.

- For *Arts Festival!*, put an X under the words that remind you of the selection.

- Repeat the same activity for the other readings.

	Informational text	Literature	Making art	Annual event
Arts Festival!				
How to Make Puppets				
The Bonnaroo Music and Arts Festival				

Discussion

1. In *Arts Festival!*, how do people prepare for the **annual** festival? How do they **participate** in it?

2. How are the festivals described in this unit similar? How are they different?

3. What different kinds of art are mentioned in the three readings?

THE BIG QUESTION What can be shown or take place at an arts festival?

> **Listening Skills**
>
> If you want to confirm your understanding, you can say, "Do you mean...?

Projects

Your teacher will help you choose one of these projects.

Written	Oral	Visual/Active
Invitation	**Group Plan**	**Advertising Poster**
Write a letter to a neighbor. Invite your neighbor to a school arts festival. Tell why it will be fun to come to the festival.	Work with a group. Plan an arts festival at your school. Make a schedule for the event. Give a formal presentation of the plan to your class.	Make a poster to advertise an arts festival. Answer the 5 W questions in your poster.
Festival Story	**Artist Interview**	**Festival Collage**
Write a story about a girl or boy who goes to an arts festival. Describe what your character sees and does at the festival.	Interview an artist in your community. Ask about what the artist has made and shown. Make a list of questions. Then tell the class about the artist's work.	Find photos of artwork on the Internet or in magazines. Make a collage of all different kinds of art that might be displayed at an arts festival.

Further Reading

For more projects visit
LongmanCornerstone.com

Tom's Cake and Kate's Lunch, Audrey McIlvain

In this Penguin Young Reader®, Tom wants to bake a cake.
He discovers that baking is hard to do. What birthday
surprises are waiting for Kate at lunchtime?

Ben's Trumpet, Rachael Isadora

Ben sees a jazz band on his way to school. He likes all
the instruments, but he likes the trumpet the most. He dreams
about being a trumpet player just like his favorite musician.

WB
223–224

Listening and Speaking Workshop

Give a How-To Presentation

You are going to write and give a how-to presentation. Then you will listen as your classmates present their how-to presentations.

❶ Prepare

A. Choose a recipe, a craft, or a game. You will present how to do it to your classmates. Then your classmates will ask you questions.

B. Think about the different steps. Then write your how-to presentation. Remember to describe what you are going to demonstrate, and then explain each step. Find props to use in the presentation.

> I'm going to show you how to take good photos with a digital camera. It's really easy. You just need a digital camera. This is my mother's camera. It's small and easy to use.
>
> First find something to take a photo of. I'm going to take a photo of our teacher, Ms. Kimball. Next, look through the camera. Make sure you can see what you're going to take a photo of...

❷ Practice

Find a partner. Practice your presentation in front of your partner. Your partner will act out or mime your instructions. Work with your partner to improve your presentation. Switch roles.

❸ Present

As you speak, do the following:

- Speak clearly and slowly.
- Show your props or other visuals.
- After your presentation, answer your classmates' questions.

As you listen, do the following:

- Listen for each step and take notes.
- Listen for ideas and information that is not stated directly.
- Think of questions to ask the speaker after the presentation.

Speaking Skills

Presentations can use formal or informal language. Choose which to use based on the purpose of the presentation and its audience.

❹ Evaluate

After you speak, answer these questions:

- ✓ Did you explain each step?
- ✓ Did working with your partner help you?

After you listen, answer these questions:

- ✓ Was the presentation formal or informal?
- ✓ Did you take notes?
- ✓ Did you ask any questions?
- ✓ Did the instructions make sense? Would you be able to explain the steps to someone else?
- ✓ Think about the general meaning of the presentation. Can you think of a title for it? Tell your idea to the class.

Listening Skills

Listen carefully for the speaker's main points and important details. Retell these ideas in your own words to confirm that you have understood them.

Writing Workshop

Write a Research Report

Writing Prompt

Write a research report that you began earlier in this unit. Present a main idea, and include facts and details to support it. Gather information from a variety of sources such as books, magazines, or online websites.

❶ Prewrite

Review the lessons in this unit. You have chosen and narrowed a topic. You have created a research plan. You have learned to paraphrase and quote directly from your sources.

A. Taking Notes

Now it is time to do your research. As you research your topic, take notes on note cards. Use one note card for each idea. Follow these steps:

- Write a label for the idea at the top of the card.
- Write your paraphrase or your quotation in the body of the card.
- Write the source, author, publisher, and page number at the bottom of the card.

You will use your cards when you plan your outline and write your report.

Here is an example of a note card:

> Important Milestones in Frida Kahlo's Life
> 1. Born in 1907 in Coyoacán, Mexico
> 2. Became ill with polio when she was six
> 3. Had a serious bus accident when she was 18
> 4. Married Mexican painter, Diego Rivera, in 1929
> Source: "Frida Kahlo." Girls Explore. 20 December 2010.
> <http://www.girls-explore.com/bios/frida-kahlo.php>

B. Making an Outline

Decide what order you would like to present the ideas in your report. Refer to your notecards. When you are ready, create an outline.

> The Life of Frida Kahlo
> A. Introduction
>   1. One of world's great artists
>   2. Painted colorful images from Mexico
>   3. Work still very popular today
> B. Frida Kahlo's life
>   1. Born in 1907, Coyoacán, Mexico
>   2. Married Diego Rivera, a famous painter
> C. Her illness and accident
>   1. Contracted polio when she was six years old
>   2. Terrible bus accident when she was 18
> D. Conclusion
>   1. Kahlo's work showed her love for Mexico
>   2. Never stopped painting; her story inspires others

❷ Draft

Use your outline to help you write a first draft.

- Begin with a paragraph that clearly presents your topic.
- Use transition words to keep your ideas flowing smoothly.
- Include citations for paraphrases and quotations.

Citing Sources Use the following examples as models to help you cite your sources correctly:

> **Book** Pearson, Anne. Ancient Greece. New York: Dorling Kindersley, 2007.
>
> **Magazine Article** Fitzgerald, Terrence. "March of the Caterpillars." Natural History September 2008: 28–33.
>
> **Internet Website** "Small but WISE." Science News for Kids. 6 January 2010. <http://www.sciencenewsforkids.org/articles/20100106/Feature1.asp>
>
> **Encyclopedia Article** Lawson, Wendy. "Antarctica." World Book Encyclopedia. 2010 ed.

❸ Revise

Read your draft. Look for places where the writing needs improvement. Use the Writing Checklist to help you. Then revise your draft.

Six Traits of Writing Checklist

✓ **Ideas**
Are all of my sentences related to the topic?

✓ **Organization**
Did I support my writing with facts?

✓ **Voice**
Does my writing show my interest in the topic?

✓ **Word Choice**
Did I choose exact, interesting words?

✓ **Sentence Fluency**
Did I vary my sentences?

✓ **Conventions**
Does my writing follow the rules of grammar, punctuation, usage, and mechanics?

Here is how Elissa revised her research report:

Elissa Chen

Frida Kahlo, Artist

Frida Kahlo was one of the world's greatest artists. She
painted pictures with bright colors and images from her
country, Mexico. We still enjoy her art today.

Frida Kahlo was born in 1907. *and she* She grew up in Mexico.
When she was twenty-one years old, she met another
famous Mexican painter named Diego Rivera. They were
married in 1929. They both loved Mexican art
and culture.

Frida Kahlo had many difficult times in her life. When
she was six years old, she became ill with a serious
disease called polio. This made one of her legs *a* weaker
than the other. When she was 18, she was in a terrible bus
accident. She had to stay in bed all the time, but she didn't
stop painting.

Frida Kahlo's work showed her love for her country.
It also showed her determination. Although she suffered many difficulties in her lifetime,
she never lost her love for life. "In spite of my long illness,"
she said, "I feel immense joy in LIVING." (Laidlaw 39)
Frida Kahlo's story has inspired people to work hard at the
things they love.

Revise to add apostrophe to show possession.

Revise to add transition word.

Revise to correct spelling error.

Revise to connect ideas.

Works Consulted List

"Frida Kahlo." Girls Explore. 20 December 2010.
    <http://www.girls-explore.com/bios/frida-kahlo.php>
Laidlaw, Jill A. Frida Kahlo New York: Franklin
    Watts, 2003.
Leveton, Deborah. "Frida Kahlo." World Book
    Encyclopedia. 2009. ed.

4 Edit

Check your work for errors. Trade papers with
a partner. Use the Peer Review Checklist to give
each other feedback.

5 Publish

Prepare a clean copy of your final draft.
Share your essay with the class.

Peer Review Checklist

✓ The main ideas and details are clear.

✓ All the information is related to the topic.

✓ Quotes are used properly.

WB
225–226

Fluency

Listen to the sentences. Pay attention to the groups of words. Read aloud.

1. The people of Red Tree work together to get ready for the arts festival.

2. People have made puppets for thousands of years, and you can too.

3. Before dancing at the Bonnaroo Music and Arts Festival, fans need to put on sunblock.

Work in pairs. Take turns reading the text below aloud for one minute. Count the number of words you read.

The Bonnaroo Music and Arts Festival happens each summer in	10
Manchester, Tennessee. More than 65,000 people come together for	19
four days of music, art, and more. Music fans can listen to	31
more than 100 bands play on many stages and tents. They	42
can choose between jazz, blues, country, rock, folk, hip-hop	51
music, and more. Kids can try out musical instruments in the	62
Kidz Jam tent, create art, and cool off on the waterslides, too.	74
Festival-goers can ride the ferris wheel and see the whole festival	86
from the top. Then they can camp out at night.	96

With your partner, find the words that slowed you down.

- Practice saying each word and then say the sentence each word is in.

- Then take turns reading the text again. Count the number of words you read.

227

Test Preparation

Taking Tests

You will often take tests that help show what you know. Follow these tips to improve your test-taking skills.

Coaching Corner

Answering Test Items That Are Cloze Items

- Cloze items ask you to fill in a blank.

- If there is a graphic, make sure you understand it.

- Read the questions and answer choices. Sometimes there is no question, just a list of words.

- Read the whole selection carefully. Try to think of words that might fit as you read.

- If you don't know what a word means, use the words around it to help you.

- In your head, read the sentence with each answer choice. Try each answer choice before choosing your answer. Choose the answer that makes the most sense.

Read the following test sample. Study the tips in the box.

WB
229–230

Read the selection. Then choose the correct words to fill in the blanks.

It's fun to make after-school __1__. These banana pops are easy and healthy. Make sure an adult helps you!

Ingredients for Banana Pops	
• 1 cup yogurt • ½ cup orange juice • 1 medium ripe banana, cut into pieces	• 6 small paper cups • blender • an adult to help

Have an adult help you measure the yogurt and juice. Have the adult cut the banana. Then put all the __2__ into a blender. Mix until smooth. Next, pour the mixture into the paper cups. Put the cups in the freezer for about 5 hours. For more variety, try using other kinds of __3__ instead of bananas. Makes 6 servings.

1 A homework
   B snacks
   C movies
   D juice

2 F chocolate
   G dishes
   H ingredients
   J bananas

3 A fruit
   B potatoes
   C bananas
   D pasta

Tips
✓ Be careful. Read the selection carefully.
✓ Try each answer choice in the blank. Choose the one that makes the most sense.

Handbook

Study Skills and Language Learning

How to Learn Language 383
How to Study. 384
How to Build Vocabulary / How to Use a Book 385
How to Use a Dictionary and Thesaurus 386
How to Take Tests 387

Viewing and Representing Information

How to Read Maps and Diagrams 388
How to Read Graphs. 389

Grammar Handbook

Parts of Speech
    Nouns and Articles 390
    Pronouns 391
    Verbs 392
    Adjectives and Adverbs. 393
    Prepositions. 394
    Conjunctions and Interjections. 395
Sentences
    Clauses and Sentences 396
    Sentence Types 396
Punctuation 397

Writing Handbook

Modes of Writing 399
The Writing Process. 400
Peer Review Checklist 402
Rubric for Writing. 404
Writing and Research 405
    Library Reference. 405
    Citing Sources. 406
    Internet Research. 408
    Information Media. 410
How to Use Technology in Writing 412

How to Learn Language

Learning a language involves listening, speaking, reading, and writing. You can use these tips to make the most of your language learning.

LISTENING

1. Listen with a purpose.
2. Listen actively.
3. Take notes.
4. Listen to speakers on the radio, television, and Internet.

SPEAKING

1. Think before you speak.
2. Speak appropriately for your audience.
3. Practice reading aloud to a partner.
4. Practice speaking with friends and family members.
5. Remember, it is okay to make mistakes.

READING

1. Read every day.
2. Use the visuals to help you figure out what words mean.
3. Reread parts that you do not understand.
4. Read many kinds of literature.
5. Ask for help.

WRITING

1. Write something every day.
2. Plan your writing before you begin.
3. Read what you write aloud. Ask yourself whether it makes sense.
4. Check for spelling and grammar mistakes.

How to Study

Here are some tips for developing good study habits.

- **Schedule a time for studying.** It is easier to develop good study habits if you set aside the same time every day to study. Once you have a study routine, it will be easier for you to find time to prepare for larger projects or tests.

- **Create a special place for studying.** Find a study area where you are comfortable and where you have everything you need for studying. If possible, choose an area that is away from telephones or television. You can play music if it helps you to concentrate.

- **Read the directions first.** Make sure you understand what you are supposed to do. Ask a partner or your teacher about anything you do not understand.

- **Preview the reading.** Look at the pictures, illustrations, and captions in the reading. They will help you understand the text.

- **Learn unfamiliar words.** Try to figure out what unfamiliar words mean by finding context clues in the reading. If you still can't figure out the meaning, use a dictionary.

- **Take notes.** Keep notes in a notebook or journal of important things you want to remember from the reading.

- **Ask questions.** Write any questions you have from the reading. Discuss them with a partner or your teacher.

How to Build Vocabulary

Use these ideas to help you remember the meanings of new words.

Keep a Vocabulary Notebook Keep a notebook of vocabulary words and their definitions. Test yourself by covering either the word or the definition.

Make Flashcards On the front of an index card, write a word you want to remember. On the back, write the meaning. Use the cards to review the words with a partner or family member.

Say the Words Aloud Use your new words in sentences. Say the sentences to a partner or a family member.

How to Use a Book

The Title Page The title page states the title, the author, and the publisher.

The Table of Contents The table of contents is at the front of a book. The page on which a chapter begins is next to its name.

The Glossary The glossary is a small dictionary at the back of a book. It will tell you the meaning of a word, and sometimes how to pronounce it. Use the glossary the same way you would use a dictionary.

The Index The index is at the back of a book. It lists subjects and names that are in the book, along with page numbers where you can find information.

The Bibliography The bibliography at the back of a book or chapter lets you know the books or sources where an author got information.

How to Use a Dictionary and Thesaurus

The Dictionary

You can find the **spelling**, **pronunciation**, **part of speech**, and **definitions** of words in the dictionary.

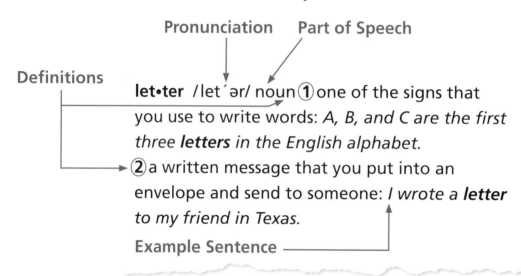

Pronunciation   Part of Speech

Definitions

let•ter /letʹər/ noun ① one of the signs that you use to write words: *A, B, and C are the first three **letters** in the English alphabet.*

② a written message that you put into an envelope and send to someone: *I wrote a **letter** to my friend in Texas.*

Example Sentence

The Thesaurus

A thesaurus is a specialized dictionary that lists **synonyms,** or words with similar meanings, and **antonyms,** or words with opposite meanings. Words in a thesaurus are arranged alphabetically. You can look up the word just as you would look it up in a dictionary.

Main entry: sad
Part of speech: adjective
Definition: unhappy
Synonyms: bitter, depressed, despairing, down, downcast, gloomy, glum, heartbroken, low, melancholy, morose, pessimistic, sorry, troubled, weeping
Antonyms: cheerful, happy

How to Take Tests

Taking tests is part of going to school. Use these tips to help you answer the kinds of questions you often see on tests.

True-False Questions

- If a statement seems true, make sure it is *all* true.
- The word *not* can change the meaning of a statement.
- Pay attention to words such as *all*, *always*, *never*, *no*, *none*, and *only*. They often make a statement false.
- Words such as *generally*, *much*, *many*, *sometimes*, and *usually* often make a statement true.

Multiple Choice Questions

- Try to answer the question before reading the choices. If your answer is one of the choices, choose it.
- Eliminate answers you know are wrong.
- Don't change your answer unless you know it is wrong.

Matching Questions

- Count each group to see whether any items will be left over.
- Read all the items before you start matching.
- Match the items you know first.

Fill-In-the-Blank Questions or Completions

- Read the question or incomplete sentence carefully.
- Look for clues in the question or sentence that might help you figure out the answer.
- If you are given possible answers, cross each out as you use it.

Short Answers and Essays

- Take a few minutes to organize your thoughts.
- Give only the information that is asked for.
- Answer as clearly as possible.
- Leave time to proofread your response or essay.

How to Read Maps and Diagrams

Informational texts often use maps, diagrams, graphs, and charts. These tools help illustrate and explain the topic.

Maps

Maps show the location of places such as countries, states, and cities. They can also show where mountains, rivers, lakes, and streets are located. A compass rose on the map shows which way is north. A scale shows how miles or kilometers are represented on the map.

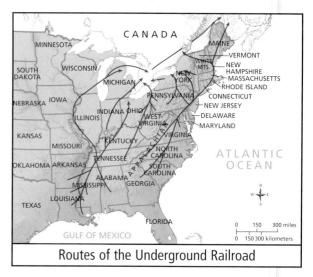

Routes of the Underground Railroad

Diagrams

Diagrams are drawings that explain things or show how things work. Some diagrams show pictures of how objects look on the outside or on the inside. Others show the different steps in a process.

This diagram shows the steps of the Scientific Method. It helps you understand the order and importance of each step.

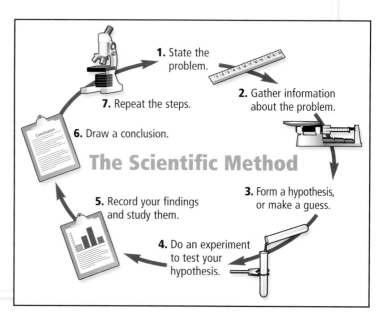

1. State the problem.
2. Gather information about the problem.
3. Form a hypothesis, or make a guess.
4. Do an experiment to test your hypothesis.
5. Record your findings and study them.
6. Draw a conclusion.
7. Repeat the steps.

The Scientific Method

How to Read Graphs

Graphs show how two or more kinds of information are related or alike. Three common kinds of graphs are **line graphs**, **bar graphs**, and **circle graphs**.

Line Graph

A **line graph** shows how information changes over a period of time. This line graph explains how the Native American population in Central Mexico changed over 100 years.

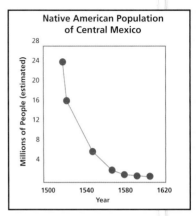

Bar Graphs

We use **bar graphs** to compare information. For example, this bar graph compares the populations of the 13 United States in 1790.

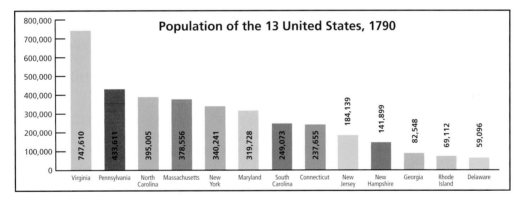

Circle Graphs

A **circle graph** is sometimes called a pie chart because it looks like a pie cut into slices. Circle graphs are used to show how different parts of a whole compare to each other.

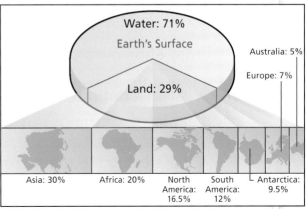

389

Parts of Speech

In English there are nine **parts of speech**: nouns, articles, pronouns, verbs, adjectives, adverbs, prepositions, conjunctions, and interjections.

Nouns

Nouns name people, places, or things.

A **common noun** is a general person, place, or thing.

> person   thing   place
> The **student** brings a **notebook** to **class**.

A **proper noun** is a specific person, place, or thing.

> person   place   thing
> **Joe** went to **Paris** and saw the **Eiffel Tower**.

Articles

Indefinite articles are *a* or *an*. They refer to a person, place, or thing.

Use *an* before a word that begins with a vowel sound.

> I have **an** idea.

Use *a* before a noun that begins with a consonant sound.

> May I borrow **a** pen?

The is called a **definite article**. Use *the* to talk about specific people, places, or things.

> Please bring me **the** box from your room.

Pronouns

Pronouns are words that take the place of nouns or proper nouns.

proper noun   pronoun **Ana** is not home. **She** is babysitting.

	Subject Pronouns	Object Pronouns
Singular	I, you, he, she, it	me, you, him, her, it
Plural	we, you, they	us, you, them

A **subject pronoun** replaces the subject of a sentence. A **subject** is who or what a sentence is about.

subject   subject pronoun (singular) **Dan** is a student. **He** goes to school every day.

Object pronouns replace a noun or proper noun that is the object of a verb. An **object** receives the action of a verb.

object   object pronoun (singular) Lauren gave **Ed** the notes. Lauren gave **him** the notes.

Possessive pronouns replace nouns or proper nouns. They show who owns something.

	Possessive Pronouns
Singular	mine, yours, hers, his
Plural	ours, yours, theirs

Verbs

Verbs express an action or a state of being.

An **action verb** tells what someone or something does or did.

Verbs that Tell Actions You Can See	Verbs that Tell Actions You Cannot See
dance swim	know sense

A **linking verb** shows no action. It links the subject with another word that describes the subject.

Examples of Linking Verbs		
look	smell	is
are	appear	seem

A helping verb comes before the main verb. They add to a verb's meaning.

	Helping Verbs
Forms of the verb *be*	am, was, is, were, are
Forms of the verb *do*	do, did, does
Forms of the verb *have*	have, had, has
Other helping verbs	can, must, could, have (to), should, may, will, would

Adjectives

Adjectives describe nouns. An adjective usually comes before the noun it describes.

tall grass   **big** truck

An adjective can come *after* the noun it describes. This happens in these kinds of sentences.

The bag is **heavy**. The books are **new**.

Adverbs

Adverbs describe the action of verbs. They tell *how* an action happens. Adverbs answer the question *Where?, When?, How?, How much?,* or *How often?*

Many adverbs end in *-ly*.

easily   slowly

Some adverbs do not end in *-ly*.

seldom   fast   very

In this sentence, the adverb *everywhere* modifies the verb *looked*. It answers the question *Where?*

verb   adverb
Nicole looked **everywhere** for her book.

Prepositions

Prepositions show time, place, and direction.

Time	Place	Direction
after	above	across
before	below	down

In this sentence, the preposition *above* shows where the bird flew. It shows place.

preposition
A bird flew **above** my head.

In this sentence, the preposition *across* shows direction.

preposition
The children walked **across** the street.

A **prepositional phrase** starts with a preposition and ends with a noun or pronoun. In this sentence, the preposition is *near* and the noun is *school*.

prepositional phrase
The library is **near the new school**.

Conjunctions

A **conjunction** joins words, groups of words, and whole sentences. Common conjunctions include *and*, *but*, and *or.*

The conjunction *and* joins two proper nouns: *Allison* and *Teresa.*

> proper   proper
> noun   noun
> Allison **and** Teresa are in school.

The conjunction *or* joins two prepositional phrases: *to the movies* and *to the mall.*

> ⌐prepositional¬   ⌐prepositional¬
>   phrase   phrase
> They want to go to the movies **or** to the mall.

The conjunction *but* joins two independent clauses.

> ⌐───independent clause───¬   ⌐───independent clause───¬
> Alana baked the cookies, **but** Eric made the lemonade.

Interjections

Interjections are words or phrases that express emotion.

Interjections that express strong emotion are followed by an exclamation point.

> **Wow!** Did you see that catch?

A comma follows interjections that express mild emotion.

> **Gee**, I'm sorry that your team lost.

Sentences

Clauses

Clauses are groups of words with a subject and a verb.

- An **independent clause** can stand on its own as a complete sentence.
- A **dependent clause** cannot stand alone as a complete sentence.

Sentences

A simple sentence is an independent clause. It has a subject and a verb.

> subject   verb
> The dog barked.

A **compound sentence** is made up of two or more simple sentences, or independent clauses.

> ┌──── independent clause ────┐   ┌── independent clause ──┐
> The band has a lead singer, **but** it needs a drummer.

Sentence Types

Declarative sentences are statements. They end with a period.

> We are going to the beach on Saturday.

Interrogative sentences are questions. They end with a question mark.

> Will you come with us?

Imperative sentences are commands. They end with a period or an exclamation point.

> Put on your life jacket. Now jump in the water!

Exclamatory sentences express strong feeling. They end with an exclamation point.

> I swam all the way from the boat to the shore!

Punctuation

End Marks

End marks come at the end of sentences. There are three kinds of end marks: periods, question marks, and exclamation points.

Periods

- Use a period to end a statement (declarative sentence).
- Use a period to end a command or request (imperative sentence).
- Use a period after a person's initial or abbreviated title.
- Use a period after abbreviations.

Question Marks and Exclamation Points

- Use an exclamation point to express strong feelings.
- Use a question mark at the end of a question.

Commas

Commas separate parts of a sentence or phrase.

- Use a comma to separate two independent clauses linked by a conjunction.
- Use commas to separate the parts in a series. A series is a group of three or more words, phrases, or clauses.
- Use a comma to set off introductory words or phrases.
- Use commas to set off an interrupting word or phrase.
- Use a comma to set off a speaker's quoted words.
- Use commas to set off the name of the person being addressed in a letter or speech.

Semicolons and Colons

Semicolons can connect two independent clauses. Use them when the clauses are closely related in meaning or structure.

Colons introduce a list of items or important information. Also use a colon to separate hours and minutes when writing the time.

Quotation Marks

Quotation marks set off direct quotations, dialogue, and some titles.

- Commas and periods always go inside quotation marks.
- If a question mark or exclamation point is not part of the quotation, it goes outside the quotation marks.
- Use quotation marks to set off what people say in a dialogue.
- Use quotation marks around the titles of short works of writing.

Apostrophes

Apostrophes can be used with singular and plural nouns to show ownership or possession. To form the possessive, follow these rules:

- For singular nouns, add an apostrophe and an *s*.
- For singular nouns that end in *s*, add an apostrophe and an *s*.
- For plural nouns that do not end in *s*, add an apostrophe and an *s*.
- For plural nouns that end in *s*, add an apostrophe.
- Apostrophes are also used in contractions, to show where a letter or letters have been taken away.

Capitalization

There are five main reasons to use capital letters:

- to begin a sentence
- to write the pronoun *I*
- to write the names of proper nouns
- to write a person's title
- to write the title of a work (artwork, written work)

Modes of Writing

Narrative Writing is used to tell a story. Here are some types of narrative writing.

- Autobiography is the story of a person's life, told by the person.
- Biography is the story of a person's life told by another person.
- A short story is a short fictional narrative.

Descriptive Writing paints a picture of a person, place, thing, or event.

Expository Writing gives information or explains something. Here are some types of expository writing.

- Compare and Contrast writing analyzes the similarities and differences between two or more things.
- Cause and Effect writing explains why something happened and what happens as a result.
- Problem and Solution writing describes a problem and offers one or more solutions to it.
- How-to writing explains how to do or make something.

Persuasive Writing is writing that tries to convince people to think or act in a certain way.

Functional Writing is writing for real-world uses. Here are some types of functional writing.

- You might fill out a form to sign up for lessons, take a field trip, or apply for a library card.
- You might create an invitation to a holiday party.

The Writing Process

The writing process is a series of steps that helps you write clearly.

Step 1: Prewrite

When you prewrite, you explore ideas and choose a topic. You identify your audience, and you choose your purpose for writing.

To choose a topic, try one or more of these strategies.
- **List** many ideas that you might want to write about.
- **Freewrite** about some ideas for five minutes.
- **Brainstorm** a list of ideas with a partner.

To identify your audience, think about who will read your writing. What do they already know? What do you need to explain?

To identify your purpose for writing, ask:
- Do I want to entertain my audience?
- Do I want to inform my audience?
- Do I want to persuade my audience?

Now, decide on the best form for your writing. Gather and organize the details that will support your topic.

Step 2: Draft

You start writing in this step. Put your ideas into sentences. Put your sentences into paragraphs. Begin to put your paragraphs in order. Don't worry too much about grammar and spelling. You will have a chance to correct any errors later.

Step 3: Revise

This is the time to look at your ideas and the organization of your writing. Read your first draft. Ask yourself:

- Are the ideas presented in the best order?
- Is there a clear beginning, middle, and end?
- Does each paragraph have a main idea and supporting details?

Decide what changes you will make. Then revise your draft.

Step 4: Edit/Proofread

This is the time to look at word choice, sentence fluency, and writing conventions. Reread your paper. Proofread for mistakes in spelling, grammar, and punctuation. Correct any mistakes you find.

When you edit and proofread your draft, use these proofreading marks to mark the changes.

Editing/Proofreading Marks		
To:	**Use This Mark:**	**Example:**
add something	∧	We ate rice, bean$_\wedge^s$ and corn.
delete something	ℒ	We ate rice, beans, and corns.
start a new paragraph	¶	¶ We ate rice, beans, and corn.
add a comma	⌄	We ate rice, beans⌄and corn.
add a period	⊙	We ate rice, beans, and corn⊙
switch letters or words	∼	We ate rice, baehs, and corn.
change to a capital letter	a̲	we ate rice, beans, and corn.
change to a lowercase letter	A̸	WE ate rice, beans, and corn.

Peer Review Checklist

Ideas

☐ Is the content interesting and thoughtful?

☐ Is the main idea clearly stated?

☐ Are the main ideas supported by facts and details?

☐ Do the ideas flow from one to the next?

Organization

☐ Are the ideas in an order that makes sense?

☐ Are the ideas connected by transitions and other connecting words?

Voice

☐ Does the writing have energy and personality?

Word Choice

☐ Has the writer chosen precise words?

Sentence Fluency

☐ Do the sentences flow smoothly?

☐ Are the sentences varied in type and length?

Conventions

☐ Do the subjects of sentences agree with the verbs?

☐ Do the pronouns agree with the words they refer to?

☐ Are the verb tenses appropriate and consistent?

☐ Is the possessive case (apostrophe -s) used correctly?

☐ Are negatives and contractions used correctly?

☐ Are the punctuation and capitalization correct?

☐ Is the writing free of spelling errors?

Step 5: Publish

Once you have revised and proofread your paper, share it with others. Look at these publishing ideas.

- Post your paper on the bulletin board.
- Photocopy your paper. Hand it out to your classmates and family members.
- Attach it to an email and send it to friends.
- Send it to a school newspaper or magazine for possible publication.

Once you have shared your work with others, you may want to put it in your portfolio. A portfolio is a folder or envelope in which you keep your writing. If you keep your work in a portfolio, you can look at what you have written over a period of time. This will let you see if your writing is improving. It will help you become a better writer.

Build Your Portfolio

You may want to keep your completed writing in your portfolio. It is a good idea to keep your drafts, too. Keep comments you receive from your teacher or writing partner, as well.

Reflect on Your Writing

Make notes on your writing in a journal. Write how you felt about what you wrote. Use these questions to help you get started.

- What new things did you learn about your topic?
- What helped you organize the details in your writing?
- What helped you revise your writing?
- What did you learn about yourself as you wrote?

Rubric for Writing

A rubric is a tool that helps you assess, or evaluate, your work. This rubric shows specific details for you to think about when you write. The scale ranges from 4 to 1, with 4 being the highest score and 1 being the lowest.

4	Writing is clearly focused on the task.
	Writing is well organized. Ideas follow a logical order.
	Main idea is fully developed and supported with details.
	Sentence structure is varied. Writing is free of fragments.
	There are no errors in writing conventions.
3	Writing is focused, with some unnecessary information.
	There is clear organization, with some ideas out of order.
	The main idea is supported, but development is uneven.
	Sentence structure is mostly varied, with some fragments.
	Writing conventions are generally followed.
2	Writing is related to the task but lacks focus.
	Organization is not clear. Ideas do not fit well together.
	There is little or no support for the main idea.
	No variation in sentence structure. Fragments occur often.
	Frequent errors in writing conventions.
1	The writing is generally unfocused.
	There is little organization or development.
	There is no clear main idea.
	Sentence structure is unvaried. There are many fragments.
	Many errors in writing conventions and spelling.

Writing and Research

Sometimes when you write, you need to do research to learn more information about your topic. You can do research in the library, on the Internet, and by viewing or listening to information media.

Library Reference

Encyclopedias contain basic facts, background information, and suggestions for additional research.

Biographical references provide brief life histories of famous people in many different fields.

Almanacs contain facts and statistics about many subjects, including government, world history, geography, entertainment, business, and sports.

Periodicals are past editions of magazines. Use a periodical index to find articles on your topic.

Vertical files contain pamphlets on a wide variety of topics.

Electronic databases provide quick access to information on many topics.

Citing Sources

When you do research, you read what other people wrote. The material you research is called the source or reference. When you tell who wrote the material, this is called citing the source. It is important to cite each source you use when you write.

In your paper, note each place in which you use a source. At the end of the paper, provide a list that gives details about all your sources. A bibliography and a works cited list are two types of source lists.

- A **bibliography** provides a listing of all the material you used during your research.

- A **works cited list** shows the sources you have quoted in your paper.

Plagiarism

Plagiarism is presenting someone else's words, ideas, or work as your own. If the idea or words are not yours, be sure to give credit by citing the source in your work. It is a serious offense to plagiarize.

Look at the chart of the Modern Language Association (MLA). Use this format for citing sources. This is the most common format for papers written by middle and high school students, as well as college students.

MLA Style for Listing Sources

Book	Pyles, Thomas. *The Origins and Development of the English Language*. 2nd ed. New York: Harcourt Brace Jovanovich, Inc., 1971.
Signed article in a magazine	Gustaitis, Joseph. "The Sticky History of Chewing Gum." *American History* Oct. 1998: 30–38.
Filmstrips, slide programs, videocassettes, DVDs	*The Diary of Anne Frank*. Dir. George Stevens. Perf. Millie Perkins, Shelly Winters, Joseph Schildkraut, Lou Jacobi, and Richard Beymer. Twentieth Century Fox, 1959.
Internet	*National Association of Chewing Gum Manufacturers*. 19 Dec. 1999. <http://www.longmancornerstone.com> [Indicate the date you found the information.]
Newspaper	Thurow, Roger. "South Africans Who Fought for Sanctions Now Scrap for Investors." *Wall Street Journal* 11 Feb. 2000.
Personal interview	Smith, Jane. Personal interview. 10 Feb. 2000.

Internet Research

The Internet is an international network of computers. The World Wide Web is a part of the Internet that lets you find and read information.

To do research on the Internet, you need to open a search engine. Type in a keyword on the search engine page. **Keywords** are words or phrases on the topic you want to learn about. For example, if you are looking for information about your favorite musical group, you might use the band's name as a keyword.

To choose a keyword, write a list of all the words you are considering. Then choose a few of the most important words.

Tips
- Spell the keywords correctly.
- Use the most important keyword first, followed by the less important ones.
- Open the pages at the top of the list first. These will usually be the most useful sources.

⟳ How to Evaluate Information from the Internet

When you do research on the Internet, you need to be sure the information is correct. Use the checklist to decide if you can trust the information on a Web site.

✓ Look at the address bar. A URL that ends in "edu" is connected to a school or university. A URL that ends in "gov" means it is a site posted by a state or federal government. These sites should have correct information.

✓ Check that the people who write or are quoted on the site are experts, not just people telling their ideas or opinions.

✓ Check that the site is free of grammatical and spelling errors. This is often a hint that the site was carefully designed and researched.

✓ Check that the site is not trying to sell a product or persuade people.

✓ If you are not sure about using a site as a source, ask an adult.

Information Media

Media is all the organizations that provide news and information for the public. Media includes television, radio, and newspapers. This chart describes several forms of information media.

Types of Information Media	
Television News Program	• Covers current news events • Gives information objectively
Documentary	• Focuses on one topic of social interest • Sometimes expresses controversial opinions
Television Newsmagazine	• Covers a variety of topics • Entertains and informs
Radio Talk Show	• Covers some current events • Offers a place for people to express opinions
Newspaper Article	• Covers one current event • Gives details and background about the event
Commercial	• Presents products, people, or ideas • Persuades people to buy or take action

How to Evaluate Information from Various Media

Because the media presents large amounts of information, it is important to learn how to analyze this information. Some media sources try to make you think a certain way instead of giving you all the facts. Use these techniques to figure out whether you can trust information from the media.

✓ Sort facts from opinions. A fact is a statement that can be proven true. An opinion is how someone feels or thinks about something. Make sure any opinions are supported by facts.

✓ Be aware of the kind of media you are watching, reading, or listening to. Is it news or a documentary? Is it a commercial? What is its purpose?

✓ Watch out for bias. **Bias** is when the source gives information from only one point of view. Try to gather information from several points of view.

✓ Discuss what you learn from different media with your classmates or teachers. This will help you determine if you can trust the information.

✓ Read the entire article or watch the whole program before reaching a conclusion. Then, develop your own views on the issues, people, and information presented.

How To Use Technology in Writing

Writing on a Computer

You can write using a word processing program. This will help you when you follow the steps in the Writing Process.

- When you write your first draft, save it as a document.
- As you type or revise, you can move words and sentences using the cut, copy, and paste commands.
- When you proofread, you can use the grammar and spell check functions to help you check your work.

Keeping a Portfolio

Create folders to save your writing in. For example, a folder labeled "Writing Projects—September" can contain all of the writing you do during that month.

Save all the drafts of each paper you write.

Computer Tips

- Rename each of your revised drafts using the SAVE AS function. For example, if your first draft is "Cats," name the second draft "Cats2."
- If you share your computer, create a folder for only your work.
- Always back up your portfolio on a server or a CD.

Glossary

advertise ▶ celebrate

A
---

advertise make people aware of and interested in an event or product (p. 324)

affect produce a change (p. 88)

alternative different from something else (p. 356)

amazing very surprising and exciting (p. 136)

annual happening every year (p. 326)

appreciate like or understand the value of something (p. 138)

artists people who paint pictures, write music, etc. (p. 354)

assign give a duty or task (p. 262)

attitude a way of thinking (p. 88)

B
---

bark the outer covering of a tree (p. 276)

benefit helped by (p. 198)

bicycles vehicles with two wheels that you sit on and ride by moving your legs (p. 196)

billions at least twice more than the number 1,000,000,000 (p. 260)

booths places at markets or fairs, where you can buy things, play games, or find information (p. 354)

brighter more sunny; having more light (p. 86)

butterfly insect that has large wings with bright colors on them (p. 166)

buttons small round objects that you push through a hole to fasten (p. 338)

C
---

camels animals with long necks and one or two humps on their backs (p. 136)

camouflage act of hiding something by making it look the same as the things around it (p. 152)

canoe narrow, light boat that you move using a paddle (p. 276)

caterpillar young form of some insects, that looks like a worm with many tiny legs (p. 166)

caves hollow places under the ground or in the side of a mountain (p. 136)

celebrate have a special meal or party because of a particular event (p. 38)

413

clouds masses of very small drops of water floating in the sky (p. 86)

company a person or people you are with (p. 38)

consist of be made up of (p. 262)

continents the large areas of land on Earth, such as Africa, Europe, and Australia (p. 260)

contribute give something (p. 40)

cocoon a silk cover some insects make to protect themselves while they are growing (p. 166)

costume clothes worn for a special reason, or that represent a country or time in history (p. 230)

craters round holes in the ground made by something that has fallen or exploded on them (p. 260)

create make something (p. 24)

crowd large groups of people (p. 38)

dessert sweet food that you eat at the end of a meal (p. 22)

dinner main meal of the day, usually eaten in the evening (p. 72)

donate give something to a person or organization that needs help (p. 196)

enable make someone or something able to do something (p. 154)

environment world of land, sea, and air that something lives in (p. 154)

festival a time of celebration; a program of cultural events (p. 324)

flight trip in an airplane or space craft (p. 290)

flower part of the plant that has the seeds and is brightly colored (p. 8)

focus pay attention to (p. 74)

fold bend a piece of paper or cloth so that one part covers the other (p. 22)

friend person you like and trust very much (p. 22)

garden piece of land where flowers or vegetables are grown around a house or in a public place (p. 104)

gathers comes together in a group (p. 38)

goal something you want to achieve (p. 356)

H

habitats natural places where plants or animals live (p. 152)

habits things that you always do, often without thinking about it (p. 136)

handprints marks on a surface that are made by a hand or hands (p. 276)

hatch come out of an egg (p. 166)

helmets hard hats that cover and protect your head (p. 196)

I

identify tell what something is (p. 74)

illustrate show; make something clear by giving examples (p. 138)

immigrate enter another country in order to live there (p. 292)

imply say something in an indirect way (p. 232)

insect very small creature such as a fly, that has six legs (p. 152)

instinct natural ability to behave in a particular way without having to think about it or learn it (p. 214)

instruments objects used for making music (p. 354)

interact communicate; talk to other people and work together with them (p. 106)

item single piece or thing (p. 10)

L

lab room or building in which a scientist works (p. 214)

leaf one of the flat green parts of a plant or tree that grow out of branches or a stem (p. 166)

luck good and bad things that happen to you by chance (p. 8)

M

mail letters and packages that you send or receive (p. 8)

mask something that covers all or part of your face (p. 230)

method a way of doing something (p. 216)

mix put different things together to make something new; join together (p. 22)

moth insect like a butterfly that flies at night (p. 152)

musicians people who play musical instruments very well or as a job (p. 354)

neat very good or pleasant (p. 8)

neighborhood small area of a town and the people who live there (p. 104)

normally most of the time (p. 198)

observe watch someone or something carefully (p. 290)

occurs happens; takes place (p. 168)

outcome the final result of a meeting, process, etc. (p. 106)

painting painted picture (p. 230)

participate be involved in (p. 326)

patterns arrangements of shapes, lines, or colors (p. 152)

perform do something to amuse people (p. 354)

phenomenon something we can observe, or see; something that is out of the ordinary (p. 278)

plains large areas of flat lands (p. 136)

planets large objects in space like Earth that move around a star such as the sun (p. 260)

plants living things that have leaves and roots (p. 104)

prey animal that is hunted and eaten by another animal (p. 152)

proof facts that prove something is true (p. 214)

puppets small figures of people or animals that you can move by pulling the strings, or by putting your hand inside them (p. 338)

purchase buy (p. 10)

quilt soft thick cover for a bed (p. 230)

rainbow large curve of different colors that appears in the sky after it rains (p. 276)

reflection what you see in a mirror or similar surface (p. 72)

required something needed (p. 340)

reverse backward; opposite way (p. 340)

roars makes a deep loud noise (p. 72)

robe long loose piece of clothing that covers most of your body (p. 230)

rotates turns around a fixed point (p. 260)

S

satellite object sent into space to receive signals from one part of the world and send them to another (p. 290)

schedule plan of what you will do and when you will do it (p. 324)

scientists people who study or work in science (p. 214)

scissors instrument with two sharp blades joined together used for cutting paper, cloth, etc. (p. 338)

seeds small grains from which new plants grow (p. 104)

significant important (p. 292)

similar almost the same, but not quite (p. 40)

soil the earth in which plants grow (p. 104)

space shuttle type of vehicle that can carry people into space and then return to Earth to be used again (p. 290)

spacewalks moving around outside a space craft while in space (p. 290)

sphere solid round shape like a ball (p. 260)

spiders small creatures with eight legs that use threads from their bodies to make webs (p. 86)

stapler tool used for putting in staples to hold pieces of paper together (p. 338)

street a road in a town or city with buildings next to it (p. 8)

stronger having more power or force (p. 86)

supplies things that are needed to carry out a task or activity (p. 324)

symbol something that stands for an idea (p. 232)

T

tadpole small creature that lives in the water and becomes a frog or toad (p. 166)

task job that must be done (p. 24)

teepee round tent used by some Native Americans (p. 230)

theory unproven idea that explains something (p. 216)

tool thing that helps you build or repair other things (p. 214)

traditional following ideas or methods that have existed for a long time (p. 278)

transform completely change (p. 168)

volunteers people who offer to do things without expecting to be paid (p. 196)

webs nets of sticky thin threads made by spiders (p. 86)

weekend Saturday and Sunday (p. 38)

well a deep hole in the ground from which water is taken (p. 72)

yarn thick thread used by someone to knit something (p. 338)

418

Index

420

421

422

Credits

TEXT CREDITS: Vivian Binnamin. "Cool Hector" by Vivian Binnamin. **Mary Ann Hoberman**. "A Year Later" by Mary Ann Hoberman. Printed by Permission.

ILLUSTRATORS: Ellen Joy Sasaki 12–17 **Laurie Keller** 26–33 **Kathryn Mitter** 43–46, 50, 341 **Aleksey and Olga Ivanov** 107 **Tim Haggerty** 76–81, 85 **Stephen Alcorn** 89–97, 99, 101 **Sarah Dillard** 142-143 **Laura Jacobsen** 218–221, 224 **Johnnee Bee** 264–269 **Joel Nakamura** 280–284 **Nathan Hale** 293, 295–297, 303

COVER: Will Terry

ICONS: Bill Melvin

LETTER LOGOS: Jan Bryan-Hunt

UNIT 1 2–3 Digital Vision/Getty Images; 5 top left, Parema/iStockphoto; 5 top right, SuperStock RF/SuperStock; 5 bottom left, Tatiana Belova/Shutterstock; 5 bottom right, prism68/Shutterstock; 6 bottom left, Robert W Ginn/PhotoEdit Inc.; 6 top right, © Tony Arruza/CORBIS; 6 bottom right, © Blend Images/Shutterstock; 7 top left, Alan Evrard/Robert Harding World Imagery; 7 bottom left, © David Turnley/CORBIS; 7 top right, © Jon Hicks/CORBIS; 7 bottom right, © Blend Images/Shutterstock; 8 top, Michael Newman/PhotoEdit Inc.; 8 bottom, © Elenathewise/Fotolia; 9 top, © Jim Cummins/CORBIS; 9 middle, Canstock Images/Alamy Images; 10 Golden Pixels LLC/Shutterstock; 19 konradlew/iStockphoto; 21 Orange Line Media/Shutterstock; 22 top, Ian O'Leary/Dorling Kindersley Media Library;

23 top, Walter Hodges/Getty Images Inc.-Stone Allstock; 23 bottom, Myrleen Ferguson Cate/PhotoEdit Inc.; 24 Francisco Romero/iStockphoto; 25 Pearson Scott Foresman; 37 PT Images/iStockphoto; 38 top, Myrleen Ferguson Cate/PhotoEdit Inc.;

39 top, Deborah Davis/PhotoEdit Inc.; 39 bottom, Tony Freeman/PhotoEdit Inc.; 40 Wendy Shiao/iStockphoto; 48 top left, © Blend Images/Shutterstock; 48 top right, Cleve Bryant/PhotoEdit, Inc. ; 48 middle left, Michael Newman/PhotoEdit, Inc.; 48 middle, Michael Newman/PhotoEdit, Inc.; 48 middle right, Tony Freeman/PhotoEdit, Inc.; 48 bottom left, Tony Freeman/PhotoEdit, Inc.; 48 bottom right, David Mager/Pearson Learning Photo Studio; 49 top left, © Catalin Petolea/Shutterstock; 49 top right, © Arvind Balarman/Shutterstock; 49 middle, Tony Freeman/PhotoEdit, Inc.; 49 bottom left, Michael Newman/PhotoEdit, Inc.; 49 bottom right, © Rob Marmion/Shutterstock; 53 Biliana Rakocevic/iStockphoto; 55 Photos.com, a division of Getty Images; 59 Micropix/Dreamstime; 62 Mariya Bibikova/iStockphoto; 65 Francesco Ridolfi/iStockphoto.

UNIT 2 66-67 Jonathan Nourok/PhotoEdit Inc.; 66 bottom left, Steve Cole/iStockphoto; 69 top left, Scott Montgomery/Getty Images Inc.–Stone Allstock; 69 top right, David Mager/Pearson Learning Photo Studio; 69 bottom left, Silver Burdett Ginn; 69 bottom right, Lawrence Migdale/Pix; 70 top left, Getty Images Inc./Hulton Archive Photos; 70 bottom left, Ron Giling/Lineair/Peter Arnold Inc.; 70 top right, Philip Gatward/Dorling Kindersley Media Library; 70 bottom right, Adam Buchanan/Danita Delimont Photography; 71 top left, Michael Newman/PhotoEdit, Inc.; 71 bottom left, © Wolfgang Kaehler/CORBIS; 71 top right, © Martin Rogers/CORBIS; 71 bottom right, Gary Braasch Photography; 72 top right, Dorling Kindersley Media Library; 72 top left, Jonelle Weaver/Getty Images, Inc./Taxi; 72 top middle, Ian OíLeary/Dorling Kindersley Media Library; 72 top middle right, © Owen Franken/CORBIS; 72 middle right, © Joe Sachs/CORBIS/PunchStock; 72 bottom, © Paul Prescott/Shutterstock; 73 top left, Dorling Kindersley Media Library; 73 top middle, Porterfield/Chickering/Photo Researchers, Inc.; 73 top right, Dorling Kindersley Media Library; 73 middle, Jerry Young/Dorling Kindersley Media Library; 73 bottom, Dorling Kindersley Media Library; 74 Feverpitch/Dreamstime; 75 Richard Embery/Pearson Education/PH College; 83 Savcoco/Dreamstime; 86 top right, Brian Cosgrove/ Dorling Kindersley Media Library; 86 top middle right, Brian Cosgrove/Dorling Kindersley Media Library; 86 middle, Linda Whitwam/Alamy, Newscom, Rex Active/ Dorling Kindersley Media Library; 86 bottom, Paul Harris/Getty Active/Dorling Kindersley Media Library; 87 top left, © Kevin M. McCarthy/Shutterstock; 87 top right, Scott Camazine/Photo Researchers, Inc.; 87 middle, Nuridsany et Perennou/Photo Researchers, Inc.; 87 bottom left, Spencer Grant/PhotoEdit, Inc.; 87 bottom right, © Michel Arnaud/Beateworks/CORBIS; 88 kristian sekulic/Shutterstock; 98 SBG Stock/ Pearson Education Corporate Digital Archive; 104 left, Anthony Harris/Shutterstock; 104 right, Mona Makela/iStockphoto; 106 Maria Bobrova/iStockphoto; 108-113 background, Carmen Martínez Banús/iStockphoto; 108 bottom, hsvrs/iStockphoto; 109 Steve Cole/ iStockphoto; 110 Photos.com, a division of Getty Images; 111 johnnyscriv/iStockphoto; 112 Marcel Pelletier/iStockphoto; 114 Carmen Martínez Banús/iStockphoto; 115 Laurent Renault/Shutterstock; 115 Anthony Harris/Shutterstock; 117 Marcel Pelletier/ iStockphoto; 119 Nancy Louie/iStockphoto; 120 Anthony Harris/Shutterstock; 123 Yuri Arcurs/Dreamstime; 126 Hakoar/Dreamstime.

GRADE 3 UNIT 3 130-131 Peter Bassett/ Nature Picture Library; 130 bottom left, Tony Heald/Nature Picture Library; 130 bottom middle, John D. Cunningham/ Visuals Unlimited; 130 bottom right, © hterra_95/Fotolia; 133 left, Poznukhov Yuriy/Shutterstock; 133 center, motorolka/ Shutterstock; 133 right, Antonio Jorge Nunes/Shutterstock; 134 top left, Castaneda,

Inc., Luis/Getty Images Inc./Image Bank; 134 bottom left, David Mager/Pearson Learning Photo Studio; 134 top right, © O. Kucharski & K. Kucharska/Shutterstock; 134 bottom right, Angus Beare/ Dorling Kindersley Media Library; 135 top left, E.A. Kuttapan/ Nature Picture Library ; 135 bottom left, Nicholas DeVore/Getty Images Inc.–Stone Allstock; 135 top right, Schafer & Hill/Getty Images Inc.–Stone Allstock; 135 bottom right, © Cixous Lionel/CORBIS/Sygma; 136 top, Art Wolfe/ Danita Delimont Photography; 136 bottom, Nick Bergkessel/Photo Researchers, Inc.; 137 top, © R. Gino Santa Maria/ Shutterstock; 137 middle, William Ervin/ Photo Researchers, Inc.; 137 bottom, Jodi Cobb/National Geographic Image Collection; 138 Steve Cukrov/Shutterstock; 139 Anup Shah/Nature Picture Library; 140 Tony Heald/ Nature Picture Library; 141 top, Tony Heald/ Nature Picture Library; 141 bottom, Anup Shah/Nature Picture Library; 144 top left, Barry Mansell/Nature Picture Library; 144 top right, Chris Johns/National Geographic Image Collection; 144 bottom left, John Eastcott and Yva Momatiuk/National Geographic Image Collection; 144 bottom right, David Kjaer/Nature Picture Library; 145 top left, Ralph Wetmore/ Creative Eye/MIRA; 145 top right, © Catcher of Light, Inc./Shutterstock; 145 bottom, Jim Stamates/Getty Images Inc.– Stone Allstock; 146 Tony Heald/Nature Picture Library; 147 Chris Johns/National Geographic Image Collection; 149 Joshua Lewis/iStockphoto; 151 Jose Alberto Tejo/ Shutterstock; 153 top, ©William Manning/ CORBIS; 153 bottom, Harry Taylor/Dorling Kindersley Media Library; 154 Boris Z./ Shutterstock; 155 Andrew Darrington/ Alamy Images; 156 top, © jordiroyg/Fotolia; 156 bottom left, Norbert Rosing/Getty Images; 156 bottom right, Paul Nicklen/Getty Images; 157 top, Andrew Darrington/Alamy Images; 157 bottom, Andrew Darrington/ Alamy Images; 158 top, Joel Sartore/National Geographic Image Collection; 158 middle, Jason Edwards/National Geographic Image Collection;

425

Connection; 159 top, Roy Toft/National Geographic Image Collection; 159 bottom, John D. Cunningham/Visuals Unlimited; 160, Jason Edwards/National Geographic Image Collection; 161 Paul Nicklen/Getty Images; 163 Fedor Selivanov/Shutterstock; 165 Ra'id Khalil/Shutterstock; 166 top, John Cancalosi/Nature Picture Library; 166 [1], Kim Taylor/Dorling Kindersley Media Library; 166 [2], Kim Taylor/Dorling Kindersley Media Library; 166 [3], Kim Taylor/Dorling Kindersley Media Library; 166 [4]. Dave King/Dorling Kindersley Media Library; 166 [5], Dave King/Dorling Kindersley Media Library; 166 [6] Geoff Dann/Dorling Kindersley Media Library; 167 top, © hterra_95/Fotolia; 167 bottom, Suzanne & Joseph Collins/Photo Researchers, Inc.; 168 Ekaterina Starshaya/Shutterstock; 169 Kim Taylor/Dorling Kindersley Media Library; 170 top, J.H. Robinson/Photo Researchers; 170 Kevin Snair/iStockphoto; 171 top tab, J.H. Robinson/Photo Researchers; 171 top, © Florian Andronache/Fotolia; 171 top middle, © Yuri Kravchenko/Fotolia; 171 middle bottom, © Beth Van Trees/Fotolia; 171 bottom, Rod Planck/Photo Researchers; 172 top tab, © Eric Isselée/iStockphoto; 172 top, © djtaylor/Fotolia; 172 middle, © hterra_95/Fotolia; 172 bottom, © Eric Isselée/Fotolia; 173 Photos.com, a division of Getty Images; 174 © Hintau Aliaksei/Shutterstock; 175 Rod Planck/Photo Researchers; 177 Wolfgang Staib/Shutterstock; 179 Jill Chen/iStockphoto; 180 Wolfgang Staib/Shutterstock; 183 Carol Gering/iStockphoto; 186 Morgan Lane Photography/Shutterstock.

UNIT 4 190–191 Image100/PunchStock; 190 bottom left, Steve Gorton and Gary Ombler/Dorling Kindersley Media Library; 190 bottom right, Jacka Photography; 193 [6], © Songquan Deng/Shutterstock; 193 [3], Dorling Kindersley Media Library; 193 top left Reuben Schulz/iStockphoto; 193 center top, Photos.com, a division of Getty Images; 193 bottom left, Stephen Aaron Rees/Shutterstock; 193 bottom center, Photos.com, a division of Getty Images; 194 top left, Angela Wyant/Getty Images Inc./Stone Allstock; 194 bottom left, Scott Cunningham/Merrill Education; 194 top right, © Gideon Mendel/CORBIS; 194 bottom right, Dave Nagel/Getty Images Inc./Stone Allstock; 195 top left, Jonathan Nourok/PhotoEdit Inc.; 195 bottom left, Dorling Kindersley Media Library; 195 top right, Pablo Eder/iStockphoto; 195 bottom right, © David Turnley/CORBIS; 196 Mark Richards/PhotoEdit, Inc.; 197 top, © Michael Jenner/CORBIS; 197 bottom, B. Daemmrich/The Image Works; 198 Jane Norton/iStockphoto; 200, © Jon Feingersh/CORBIS; 201 top, Skjold Photographs; 201 bottom, © Nik Wheeler/CORBIS; 202 top, Lawrence Migdale/Pix; 202 bottom, © Mika/zefa/CORBIS; 203 top, © Heide Benser/zefa/CORBIS; 203 bottom, © CORBIS; 204 top, argus/Hartmut Schwarzbach/Peter Arnold, Inc.; 206 top, National Geographic Image Collection; 206 bottom left, Peter Downs/Dorling Kindersley Media Library; 206 bottom right, Steve Gorton and Gary Ombler/Dorling Kindersley Media Library; 207 top left, Norm Dettlaff/AP Wide World Photo 207 top right, Getty Images/Stockbyte; 207 middle, Philip Gatward/Dorling Kindersley Media Library; 207 bottom, © Glyn Jones/Corbis; 199 Skjold Photographs; 208 © Nik Wheeler/CORBIS; 209 argus/Hartmut Schwarzbach/Peter Arnold, Inc.; 211 Jane Norton/iStockphoto; 213 Gladskikh Tatiana/Shutterstock; 214 top, Steve Shott/Dorling Kindersley Media Library; 214 middle, Jane Burton/Dorling Kindersley Media Library; 214 bottom, Peter Anderson/Dorling Kindersley Media Library; 215 top, Art Resource/Schomburg Center for Research in Black Culture; 215 bottom, Michael K. Nichols/National Geographic Image Collection; 216 Photos.com, a division of Getty Images; 217 Cal Vornberger/Peter Arnold, Inc.; 222 top, Alexander Weir; 223 Gavin Hunt; 225 Alexander Weir; 227 Life Collections/iStockphoto; 229 Peter Scoones/Photo Researchers, Inc.; 230 top, Dave King/Dorling Kindersley Media Library;

230 middle top, (c) Fine Art Photographic Library/CORBIS; 230 middle bottom, Rafael Macia/Photo Researchers, Inc.;

231 top, The Bridgeman Art Library International; 231 bottom, Gary Ombler/Dorling Kindersley Media Library; 232 FloridaStock/Shutterstock; 233 © Irafael/Shutterstock; 234 © Sam Chadwick/Shutterstock; 235 top right, © Sally Scott/Shutterstock; 235 top left, Charles Butzin III/Shutterstock; 235 bottom left, Justin Williford/Shutterstock; 235 bottom right, Sally Scott/Shutterstock; 236 bottom left, Denver Art Museum; 236 top left, © Irafael/Shutterstock; 236 top right, Silver Burdett Ginn; 236 bottom right, Jacka Photography; 237 top left, © CLM/Shutterstock; 237 top right, © Mikhail Olykainen/Shutterstock; 238 © Hannamariah/Shutterstock; 239 Denver Art Museum; 241 Charles Butzin/iStockphoto; 243 lilly3/iStockphoto; 247 Photos.com, a division of Getty Images; 250 Michelle Malven/iStockphoto.

UNIT 5 254-255 Robert Karpa/Masterfile; 257 NASA; 262 Alexey Stiop/iStockphoto; 258 top left, John R. Foster/Photo Researchers, Inc.; 258 bottom left, Tony Freeman/PhotoEdit Inc.; 258 top right, Michael J. Doolittle/The Image Works; 258 bottom right, Richard T. Nowitz/Photo Researchers, Inc.; 259 top left, David Nunuk/Photo Researchers, Inc.; 259 bottom left, © Digital Media Pro/Shutterstock; 259 top right, Stephen Dorey/Alamy Images Royalty Free; 259 bottom right, © Pete Pahham/Shutterstock; 260 top, Peter Cade/Stone/Getty Images; 260 middle, NASA/Corbis Los Angeles; 260 bottom, Lucio Rossi/Dorling Kindersley Media Library; 261 bottom left, Mike Berceanu/Photolibrary.com; 261 bottom middle, European Space Agency/Science Photo Library/Photo Researchers, Inc.; 261 bottom right, NASA/GSFC/NOAA/USGS/Reuters/CORBIS/Reuters America LLC; 270 © Jacek Chabraszewski/Fotolia; 270 Nancy Catherine Walker/iStockphoto; 271 Neil Armstrong/The

Granger Collection; 271 NASA; 273 Vladimir Piskunov/iStockphoto; 273 Vladimir Piskunov/iStockphoto; 275 NASA; 278 NASA; 276 top left, Dorling Kindersley Media Library; 276 top middle, Pearson Education/EMG Education Management Group; 276 top right, Michael S. Lewis/National Geographic Image Collection; 276 middle, Rod Planck/Photo Researchers, Inc.; 276 bottom left, Donna Coleman/iStockphoto; 277 top, © Elena Elisseeva/Shutterstock; 277 bottom, Ira Block/National Geographic Image Collection; 279 Dorling Kindersley Media Library; 279 top, Joze Pojbic/iStockphoto; 279 bottom, Eric Isselée/iStockphoto; 285 Tom Powers; 287 Paul Morton/iStockphoto; 290 top, NASA/Finley Holiday Films/Dorling Kindersley Media Library; 290 bottom, Dorling Kindersley Media Library; 291 left, Tony Freeman/PhotoEdit Inc.; 291 right, Getty Images Inc./Stone Allstock; 292 asiseeit/iStockphoto; 300 top left, NASA/Photo Researchers, Inc.; 300 top right, NASA/Science Source/Photo Researchers, Inc.; 300 bottom left, NASA/John F. Kennedy Space Center; 300 bottom right, NASA/Goddard Laboratory for Atmospheres; 301 top left, NASA/Photo Researchers, Inc.; 301 top right, JPL/NASA Headquarters; 301 bottom, CORBIS/Bettmann; 302 NASA/Johnson Space Center; 305 Eileen Hart/iStockphoto; 308 Paul Morton/iStockphoto; 311 NASA; 314 Vladimir Piskunov/iStockphoto.

UNIT 6 318–319 Angelo Cavalli/Robert Harding World Imagery/Getty Images; 318 right, © Bill Bachmann/Index Stock Imagery; 321 left, memaggiesa/Shutterstock; 321 right, wiedzma/iStockphoto; 322 top left, Gordon Wiltsie/National Geographic Image Collection; 322 bottom left, Keren Su/Danita Delimont Photography; 322 top right, Spencer Grant/PhotoEdit Inc.; 322 bottom right, Pearson Learning Photo Studio; 323 top left, AP Wide World Photos; 323 bottom left, Angelo Cavalli/Getty Images Inc.–Image Bank; 323 top right, Odile Noel/Lebrecht Music & Arts Photo Library; 323